THE
COUNTRY DANCE BOOK

PARTS V & VI

THE

COUNTRY DANCE BOOK

PARTS V & VI

DESCRIBED BY

CECIL J. SHARP

AND

MAUD KARPELES

EP Publishing Limited
1976

Republished 1976 by EP Publishing Limited
East Ardsley, Wakefield
West Yorkshire, England

This is a reprint of Part V, first published in 1918, and Part VI, first published in 1922. Both parts were originally published by Novello & Company Limited

Corrections and additions

An undated list of corrections and additions, covering Parts II–VI, was also published by Novello and Company Limited. The items pertaining to Parts V and VI are reproduced at the end of this book.

ISBN 0 7158 1143 6

Please address all enquiries to EP Publishing Limited
(address as above)

Printed in Great Britain by
The Scolar Press Limited, Ilkley, West Yorkshire

THE
COUNTRY DANCE BOOK

PART V

CONTAINING

THE RUNNING SET

COLLECTED IN KENTUCKY, U. S. A.
AND DESCRIBED

BY

CECIL J. SHARP

AND

MAUD KARPELES

LONDON: NOVELLO AND COMPANY, Ltd.
NEW YORK: THE H. W. GRAY Co.
SOLE AGENTS FOR THE U. S. A.

TO

THE PINE MOUNTAIN
SETTLEMENT SCHOOL

CONTENTS

INTRODUCTION

In the course of our travels in the Southern Appala-chian Mountains in search of traditional songs and ballads, we had often heard of a dance, called the Running Set, but, as our informants had invariably led us to believe that it was a rough, uncouth dance, remarkable only as an exhibition of agility and physical endurance, we had made no special effort to see it. When at last we did see it performed at one of the social gatherings at the Pine Mountain Settlement School it made a profound impression upon us. We realized at once that we had stumbled upon a most interesting form of the English Country-dance which, so far as we knew, had not been hitherto recorded, and a dance, moreover, of great æsthetic value. On that occasion, the dance was sprung unexpectedly upon us by Miss Ethel de Long, and, being quite unprepared, we were unable to make any attempt to note it.

Shortly afterwards we again saw the Running Set at Hindman (Knott Co., Ky.) at an evening party especially arranged in our honour by Mr. Burnham Combs. On that occasion, however, the executants, being unaccustomed to dance together, differed so widely in their individual movements that although we were able to add very considerably to our knowledge we could do no more than make a few notes of a general character.

A few weeks later we saw the dance on two different occasions at Hyden (Leslie Co., Ky.). The first of these was organized for our benefit by Mr. Lewis and Mr. Asher and was held at Mr. Westcott's house under the most favourable conditions. The executants were picked dancers, there were no onlookers to disturb us, and we were able to note the dance with all its intricacies at our leisure, and afterwards to clear up doubtful technical points by reference to Mr. Lewis.

The second time we saw the Running Set at Hyden was at a "frolic," the sequel to a "bean-stringing," given by Mr. Lee Morgan. The guests assembled by twos and threes in the afternoon from four o'clock onwards and, on arrival, were set to work to string the beans which lay in heaps upon the floor of every room. This preliminary task occupied some hours, and it was nine o'clock before preparations for the dance were made and the "frolic" proper began. One of us took part in the first Set that was "run" that evening—the dancing continued well into the small hours—and gained thereby a practical and first-hand acquaintance with the dance which we have since found invaluable.

In the following month Mr. Sewell Williams explained to us the way in which the Running Set was danced at Quicksand (Breathitt Co., Ky.), and from him we gathered some additional figures as well as several variants of those that we had already seen and noted (see Appendix, A and B).

The version of the dance described in the following pages is that which we noted at Hyden, although in our general instructions, concerning style, etc., we have drawn very largely upon what we observed at Pine Mountain, where the dance was executed more perfectly and with greater finish than elsewhere.

The only kind of dancing other than the Running Set that we have as yet seen in the mountains is a species of step- or clog-dance, locally known as the hoe-down. We happen to know, however, that many forms of the Country-dance—*e. g.*, Square-eights and Longways dances —still survive in the Appalachians and other parts of America, and these we hope eventually to investigate and, perhaps, to publish in a second edition of this volume.

Apart from its innate beauty and its many artistic

qualities, the Running Set is especially interesting in that it represents one particular phase in the development of the Country-dance of which, hitherto, nothing has been known. It is, in a sense, a new discovery. A few words concerning the history of the Country-dance and of our sources of information regarding it will make this clear.

The English Country-dance is the lineal descendant of the May-day Round, a pagan quasi-religious ceremonial of which the May-pole dance is, perhaps, the most typical example. Except for a few stray references to the Country-dance in early literature nothing is known of its history prior to 1650, in which year the first book on the subject, Playford's *English Dancing Master*, was published. This modest little book, containing the description of 104 dances, won so great a popularity that, under the modified title of *The Dancing Master*, it ran through eighteen editions, the last of which, dated 1728, contained upwards of seven hundred dances. A critical examination of these successive editions shows that the dance degenerated very rapidly during the period covered by them, and the large number of dance-manuals subsequently issued by Walsh, Thompson, Waylett, and others furthermore proves that this decline continued during the two following centuries until, at the beginning of the present century, the only dances that remained were those—chiefly of the Longways variety—that were still being danced by the peasantry in remote country districts of England and Scotland.

Now the Running Set in its structure (with one partial exception to which reference will presently be made) and in many other important particulars differs materially from any other known form of the Country-dance. It is built on much larger lines than any other of which we have cognizance. The Promenade movements, which bind the figures together and give continuity to the dance, occur nowhere else; while The Wild Goose-chase, The California Show Basket, and Wind up the Ball Yarn are figures which hitherto have only been found in children's singing-

games.   Moreover, the forceful, emotional character of
the dance; the absence from it of all the courtesy movements, *i. e.*, the Set, the Side, the Honour, and the Arms;
the speed with which the evolutions are executed, and the
unconventional way in which the dancers comport themselves—all tend sharply to differentiate the Running Set
from the Playford dances and all other known forms of the
English Country-dance.

From these considerations we are led to infer that the
Running Set represents a stage in the development of the
Country-dance earlier than that of the dances in *The
English Dancing Master*—at any rate in the form in which
they are there recorded.

The fact, for instance, that the movements of courtesy,
which occur in almost every one of the Playford dances,
are conspicuously absent from the Running Set is of itself
the strongest testimony in favour of the priority of the
latter.   For it is extremely unlikely that these movements,
which were obviously due to the influence of the drawing-
room and reflect the formal manners and conventional
habits of the upper ranks of an organized society, could
have found their way into the dance many years before
1650.   Indeed, it might be maintained, that it was the
intrusion of these and similar movements into the Country-
dance which initiated and ultimately led to its decline.

The only dance in *The English Dancing Master* which,
in its construction, bears any resemblance to the Running
Set is Up Tails All (1st ed., 1650; *The Country Dance Book*,
Part iii).   This is a " Round for as many as will " and
consists of an Introduction and three Parts.   Each Part
contains a fresh figure, which is led successively by each
couple in turn, as in the Running Set; but there is no general movement, corresponding to the Promenade, between
the repetitions of the figure or between the Parts.   As Up
Tails All is the only Round of its kind in *The Dancing
Master* it is fair to infer that it represents a late and—in
comparison with the Running Set—a corrupt example of an

earlier and almost extinct type, rather than the forerunner of a fresh development.

The three figures, hitherto known only in children's singing games, of which mention has already been made, are one and all derived from ancient pagan ceremonials.

The California Show Basket is an adaptation to the dance of a children's singing-game, Draw a pail of water, which is a dramatic representation of several incidents connected with the ceremony of well-worship. The only one of these ritual acts which survives in the dance-figure is the passing first of the women under the arms of the men and then of the men under the arms of the women, in imitation of the creeping of the devotee under the sacred bush, which was frequently found by the side of the holy well (see Alice B. Gomme's *Traditional Games of England, etc.*, i, p. 100; ii, p. 503).

Wind up the Ball Yarn is a variant of one of the "winding up games" such as The Eller Tree, or Wind up the Bush Faggot. Games of this type originated in the custom of encircling a tree or other sacred object as an act of worship, the connection of the worshippers, by means of linked hands, with the central object, being intended to communicate life and action to it (*Traditional Games of England, etc.* i, p. 119; ii, pp. 384, 510).

The Wild Goose-chase is one of the many serpentine movements—*e. g.*, the Hey in its many forms—which are so often found in dances of religious or magical significance (*cf.* the movement in Morris Off in *The Morris Book*, 1st ed.). Lady Gomme (*Traditional Games of England, etc.*, ii, p. 511) cites an Irish custom recorded by Lady Wilde in which young men and maidens with clasped hands described curves very similar to those in the dance figure.

Wind up the Ball Yarn, it is interesting to record, has been appropriated and used very effectively by the Russians in one of their ballets.

The ring-movement around a central dancer in The Bird

in the Cage and Tucker is not unlike one of the figures
in the Scottish Eightsome-Reel (itself a Nature dance)
and is probably derived from some sacrificial ceremony.
The dancer within the ring may be the victim about to be
seized and sacrificed as in several of the Sword-dances
(*cf.* The Grenoside Sword-dance) and in the Morris Dance,
Brighton Camp (*The Morris Book*, iii, p. 55).

The fact that these indubitably ancient figures are in-
corporated as organic movements in the Running Set
and (with the exception of Tucker and The Bird in the
Cage) occur in no other recorded dance, still further
strengthens the claim that the Kentucky dance belongs to
a stage in the development of the Country-dance earlier
than that of any dance known to us.

If this contention be conceded we have next to enquire
how and at what period the Running Set found its way to
America.   Now the fact that the dance could not have
reached America before 1650 (unless it came over with the
Pilgrim Fathers in the *Mayflower!*) does not in reality con-
flict with our hypothesis, although at first sight it may
seem to do so.   For, bearing in mind the physical difficulties of communication between one part of the country
and another in the fifteenth and sixteenth centuries, it is
extremely improbable that the successive developments
of the Country-dance proceeded uniformly at one and the
same time in every part of England.

Now *The English Dancing Master* was published in
London and addressed primarily, if not exclusively, to
Londoners, or at most to those resident in the Southern
and Midland counties of England.   In what form, however, the Country-dance existed at that period in other
parts of England, we have no means of knowing, although,
as the civilization in the North has always lagged behind
that of the South, we may assume that it was of a less
advanced type.   It may be, therefore,—indeed, it is
extremely probable—that dances of the same species as
the Running Set were, in the middle of the seventeenth

century and for many years later—*i. e.*, for some while after they had been discarded or superseded in the South —still being danced in the Northern counties of England and the Scottish Lowlands, the very districts from which the forefathers of the present Southern Appalachians originally emigrated.

Although, then, we may be unable to ascribe to the Running Set a definite date, we may with some assurance claim: —that it is the sole survival of a type of Country-dance which, in order of development, preceded the Playford dance; that it flourished in other parts of England and Scotland a long while after it had fallen into desuetude in the South; and that some time in the eighteenth century it was brought by emigrants from the Border counties to America where it has since been traditionally preserved.

This explanation at any rate accords with, and follows logically from, the facts so far as they are at present known. Further investigations, however, in the Southern Highlands and in other parts of America may, perhaps, lead to the discovery of more examples of this particular type of Country-dance, and it may then become necessary to modify the theory above enunciated.

It is interesting to note that the dancers who were "men" and "women" in Playford's book have become "ladies" and "gentlemen" in the Running Set (see Appendix C) which, by the way, is also the title given to them in the eighteenth-century dance-books. The "Promenade," too, is, I take it, also an eighteenth-century expression. This adoption of an eighteenth-century nomenclature in the description of a sixteenth- or seventeenth-century dance is at first sight a little disconcerting, but it really proves no more than that the jargon of the dance travelled more quickly to the North of England than the dance movements themselves, a fact for which we have every reason to be thankful.

It is not easy to give a satisfactory derivation of Do-Si, or Do-si-do, the name by which one of the most characteristic movements of the Running Set is universally known in the mountains. The obvious explanation is that it is a corruption of the French dos-à-dos, but, if this be so, it is, of course, a misnomer because the Do-si-do of the Running Set is quite a different evolution from that which is ordinarily understood by the Back-to-back. The French derivation may, nevertheless, be the correct one, for it is quite in accordance with the habit of the mountaineer to call things by their wrong names, *e. g.*, Laurel for Rhododendron; Ivy for Laurel; Vine for Ivy; Biscuit for Scone, etc.

When the last book of English folk-dances was published—now some years ago—it looked as if the available material were at last exhausted, and that our knowledge of existing traditional dances had practically reached its limit. That further and most valuable material actually existed at that time in a country several thousand miles away from England, patiently awaiting the call of the collector, certainly did not occur to me, nor, I am sure, to any of my friends or collaborators. And even when, later on, I had penetrated into the Southern Appalachians and found the old Puritan dislike, fear, and distrust of dancing expressed in almost every log-cabin I entered, the possibility seemed more remote than ever. My surprise, then, can be imagined when, without warning, the Running Set was presented to me, under conditions, too, which immensely heightened its effect. It was danced, one evening after dark, on the porch of one of the largest houses of the Pine Mountain School, with only one dim lantern to light up the scene. But the moon streamed fitfully in lighting up the mountain peaks in the background and, casting its mysterious light over the proceedings, seemed to exaggerate the wildness and the break-neck speed of the dancers as they whirled through the mazes of the dance. There was no music, only the stampings and clappings of the onlookers, but when one of the emotional crises of the dance was reached—and this happened several times during the performance—the air seemed literally to pulsate with the rhythm of the "patters" and the tramp of the dancers' feet, while, over and above it all, penetrating through the din, floated the even, falsetto tones of the Caller, calmly and unexcitedly reciting his directions.

The scene was one which I shall not readily forget and, in the impression which it made upon me, it recalled to my mind the occasion when I first saw the Handsworth Sword-dance, a dance, with which in a curious, subtle sort of way, the Running Set has a close affinity.

Whether the dancers and others to whom this book is addressed will agree with the high estimate of the æsthetic qualities of the Running Set that I have myself formed remains to be seen, but I shall be very surprised if within a few months of its publication, the members of the English Folk Dance Society here and in England are not dancing it merrily in every one of the Society's Branches and Centres.

The dance has already been publicly performed in New York and Boston and on both occasions won the approbation, certainly of the performers and, I think, also of the spectators. A new dance, especially one so characteristic as the Running Set and so unlike any other folk-dance, was sure to strike different people in different ways. Of the many criticisms that have been expressed in my hearing. two stand out over and above the rest and seem worthy of record. The first of these was the comment of an on-looker, a school-teacher:—"Yes, it is a beautiful dance, but terribly difficult. And what's the use of it anyway? You couldn't teach it!" The other was a remark breath-lessly made by one of the executants at the conclusion of a performance:—"That's what I call a lovely dance! You needn't bother yourself about style, or anything. You have only to forget everything and let yourself go!"

C. J. S.

Hotel Algonquin,
  New York,
    Christmas, 1917.

THE STEPS

The normal step used in the Running Set is a swift, short, and exceedingly smooth Country-dance running-step, the spring from foot to foot, though never omitted, being so slight as to be scarcely noticeable. The step, indeed, is so smooth that the dancers, as we saw them, seemed at times to be moving, or gliding, on wheels. When the tempo of the dance is at its fastest, the step becomes almost indistinguishable from that of the Rapper Sword-dance.

There are no skipping or slipping-steps although, especially in the Promenades, the dancers often improvise step-variations of their own, *e. g.* kick up their heels, drag their feet lazily on the floor, or do a hoe-down step or two, *i.e.*, a heel-and-toe, shuffle, or clog-dance step.

THE MUSIC

At Hyden the accompanying music was played on the fiddle; at Hindman on the fiddle and banjo. At Pine Mountain there was no music at all.

Throughout the dance the onlookers and the performers also, when not actually dancing, should enforce the rhythm of the music by "patting," *i.e.*, alternately stamping and clapping. "Patting" is done in various ways, but the usual method is to stamp with the right foot on the strong accent and clap the hands on the weak one, the executant throwing his head back, inclining his body to the left and emphasizing the movements of feet and hands so that the rhythm may be seen as well as heard. In $\frac{6}{8}$ time the hands are usually clapped on the third and sixth quavers, but the "patter" will often strike his thighs, right hand on right thigh on the second and fifth quavers, and left hand on left thigh on the third and sixth, stamping, of course, on the first and fourth quavers.

As an accompaniment to the dance, the "patting" is almost as effective as the music; so effective, indeed, that at Pine Mountain, where the dancers were wholly dependent upon it, the absence of instrumental music was scarcely felt.

The fiddler and the banjo-player each have an assistant, a "beater," who, sitting at right-angles to the instrumentalist, "beats" the strings between the bridge and the player's left hand with two pencil-like, wooden sticks. These sticks being flexible, strike all the strings simultaneously and this produces a rhythmical, drone effect which if the "beater" is deft in his movements and skilfully varies his rhythms, adds depth to the tune and gives material aid to the dancers.

17   B

The tunes should be jig-tunes, not Country-dance airs, which are too suave and lack the insistent beat characteristic of the Running Set. The tunes we heard at Hindman, Hyden, and elsewhere were not very good ones, far inferior, for instance, to those of the English peasant-fiddlers; though the players in Kentucky generally managed, notwithstanding the melodic poverty of the tunes, to play them with such force and abandonment that they made excellent accompaniment to the dance.

It seems possible to find other airs which, while equally satisfying the requirements of the dance, shall be superior to the Kentucky tunes in melodic interest. An attempt in this direction has been made in the collection of airs (*Country Dance Tunes*, Set 9) published in connection with this volume.

As in many of the Sword-dances, the music controls the steps only and not the evolutions which may begin, or end, at any part of a musical phrase. It is desirable, however, that the dance-phrases should, whenever possible, be brought into coincidence with those of the music and, with the exercise of a little ingenuity on the part of the dancers, this can often be done, *e.g.*, in the two eight-step movements in the Grand Promenade. Some of the Figures, such as "The California Show Basket," or "Going down Town," can be danced throughout phrase by phrase with the music as accurately as in a Country-dance.

In the Running Set the instrumentalist is just an accompanist and no more. The dancers set the tempo, varying it from moment to moment at their pleasure, and these variations it is the duty of the player to follow as though he were accompanying a song.

The tunes given in the music volume may be played in any order that the accompanist pleases, and changed as often as he may elect.

THE CALLER

It is customary for one of the company, not necessarily one of the dancers, to "call" the dance as it proceeds, that is, to name the figures and describe them, movement by movement, and thus to do for the dancers what the prompter at the opera does for the singers. Normally, the "caller" recites certain prescribed verbal phrases, a mixture of prose and doggerel rhyme that in the course of time has become stereotyped (see Appendix C, p. 48). He does not always, however, restrict himself exclusively to the use of these, but will sometimes improvise remarks of his own, after the manner of the chantey-man, and crack jokes, chaff the dancers, and so forth. Mr. Taylor, who "called" the dance at Pine Mountain and was himself the leader of the dance, gave out his directions in a high, falsetto monotone which was very effective. Whether or not this is the traditional method of "calling" we have not been able to discover.

GENERAL INSTRUCTIONS

In its general effect, in the continuous movement, the periodic recurrence of circular evolutions, the short, quick step of the dancers, and, above all, in its tense, restrained emotion, the Running Set resembles the Sword-dance rather than the Country-dance with which, nevertheless, for technical and historical considerations, it must logically be classified.

The outstanding characteristic of the Running Set is the swift, lightning speed with which the figures are negotiated. Indeed, at first sight it may appear as though the dancers were wholly absorbed in the execution of the figures in the shortest possible time, regardless of manner or style. The half-turns in the Promenade, for instance, are done most perfunctorily, and never with straight arms as in the Country-dance; sometimes, indeed, the hands of the dancers will scarcely touch one another, or the man will place his hands on the shoulders or upper arms of his partner. But this apparent negation of style is quite illusory, as the critical observer will discern, and as the dancer will soon find out for himself. For, para-doxical as it may seem, it is precisely in its style—or lack of style—in the unconventional way in which the figures and evolutions are executed, that the character and, it may be added, the extraordinary charm of this unique dance lie.

It cannot be too strongly emphasized that despite the break-neck speed and the rush of it, the dance must in its every movement be performed smoothly, quietly, almost nonchalantly; in the hands of unskilled dancers it may easily degenerate into a disorderly romp.

The technical equipment needed by the dancer in

the Running Set is not to be acquired without trouble and practice. He must have a highly developed sense of direction—a step at a wrong angle may, as in the Sword-dance, throw a whole movement out of gear; great agility, combined with consummate neatness, a keen intelligence, and an instinct for thinking ahead, that is, realizing what is coming and preparing for it.

The body should be held erect, motionless, with every limb loose and relaxed, and inclined in the direction of motion, as in skating. The arms, when not actively engaged, should hang loosely by the sides, swinging naturally this way or that in rhythm with the motion of the body. This reposeful carriage, together with the swift, gliding movement already described, gave to the dancers, as we saw them at Pine Mountain, an impersonal, detached appearance, as though they were moving in a dream or under hypnotic influence.

Finally, it must never for one moment be forgotten that the Running Set is, first and last, a team-dance, and that individual proficiency will not of itself suffice without close co-operation on the part of the dancers in the co-ordination and timing of their movements.

TECHNICAL TERMS AND SYMBOLS

In the following description of movements, figures, etc., it will be necessary to make use of certain technical terms and symbols. These will now be defined.

○ = man.

⊔ = woman.

The area enclosed by the dancers is known as the *Set*, or the *General Set*.

In movements in which two couples only are engaged, the terms *contrary man* and *contrary woman* are used to denote the man or woman other than the partner.

In ring-formation, *contrary* or *contrary partner* is the woman on the left of the man, or the man on the right of the woman.

To *cross hands* the man takes the right and left hands of the woman with, respectively, his right and left hands, the right hands being above the left.

To *pass by the right* is to pass right shoulder to right shoulder; *by the left*, left shoulder to left shoulder.

When two dancers meet and pass each other they should always, unless otherwise directed, pass by the right.

To make a quarter-turn is to turn through 90°.

To make a half-turn is to turn through 180°.

To make a three-quarter turn is to turn through 270°.

To make a whole-turn is to make a complete revolution.

The terms *clockwise* and *counter-clockwise* are self-explanatory and refer to circular movements.

To *cast off* is to turn outward and dance outside the Set, or outside the area enclosed for the moment by the dancers.

To *cast back* is to make a half-turn outward and move in the opposite direction.

To *lead* or *move* is to dance forwards.

To *fall back* is to dance backwards.

The *double* is three steps, forward or backward, followed by "feet-together."

To *arm with the right*, or *arm-right*, two dancers link right arms and swing once round, clockwise.

To *arm with the left*, or *arm-left*, two dancers link left arms and swing once round, counter-clockwise.

To *turn*, two dancers face, join both hands, and swing once round, clockwise.

Hands-three, hands-four, etc. Three or more dancers, as directed, join hands, dance round in a ring, clockwise, and make one complete circuit.

Right-hands-across, or *left-hands-across*. Two couples face. The two men and the two women, joining right or left hands, as directed, dance round, clockwise, holding their hands close together, chin-high, and facing in the direction of motion.

CONSTRUCTION

The Running Set is most effective when the number of dancers is limited to four couples, although, if certain Figures be omitted, that number may be exceeded.

The performers stand in a circle, thus:—

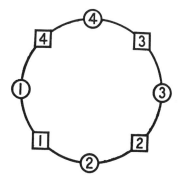

The construction of the dance is very similar to that of the Rapper Sword-dance. It consists of an Introduction, followed by an indefinite number of Parts, each of which contains its own distinctive Figure, preceded by the Grand Promenade, a circular movement in which all the dancers take part. Except in two cases (Figs. 10 and 13) the special Figure which distinguishes each Part is executed four times, led successively by each of the four couples, the Little Promenade (a shortened form of the Grand Promenade) being interposed before each repetition.

The division of the dance into Parts and Figures is quite arbitrary and is done merely for the sake of convenience and clearness. No pause, however, is made between the Parts, nor between the successive repetitions of the Figures, the dance being one continuous movement from beginning to end.

GENERAL FIGURES

Before entering upon a technical description of the several movements and Figures in their proper order, it will be as well, perhaps, first to explain certain evolutions which continually recur in the course of the dance. There are three of these:—the Grand Promenade, the Little Promenade, and the Do-si-do-and-promenade-home.

THE GRAND PROMENADE

Men turn their partners half-way round (four steps), turn their contraries (*i.e.*, the women on their left) half-way round (four steps), rejoin their partners, cross hands (right over left) and all move round the circle eight steps counter-clockwise, men on the inside (*i.e.*, on the left of their partners).

It will be found that in making the two half-turns each dancer describes a complete circle clockwise.

Without releasing hands, all reverse their direction, the men making a half-turn clockwise, the women a half-turn counter-clockwise, and move round the circle eight steps clockwise, the men being on the inside (*i.e.*, on the right of their partners).

Men turn their partners half-way round (four steps), turn their contraries half-way round (four steps), rejoin their partners, cross hands and dance round the circle with them, counter-clockwise, to places.

THE LITTLE PROMENADE

Men turn their partners half-way round (four steps), turn their contraries half-way round (four steps), rejoin their partners, cross hands and move once round, the circle with them, counter-clockwise, to places, men on the inside (*i.e.*, on the left of their partners).

Do-si-do-and-Promenade-Home

Two couples face. Men turn their partners half-way round with left hands, pass each other by the right (moving sideways, right shoulders forward, and back-to-back), turn their contraries half-way round with right hands and return to places, passing each other by the left (back-to-back, left shoulders forward). This movement, which is known as the Do-si-do, or the Do-si, is then repeated.

At the conclusion of the repetition, men turn their partners once round with left hands, cross hands with them and dance round a small circle, counter-clockwise, each couple breaking off and proceeding to its original station.

The half-turns in the Do-si-do must be executed at great speed and with bent arms, each performer describing as small a circle as possible. In crossing over between the turns the men should arch their backs and pass as closely to each other as they can.

THE DANCE

All take hands and dance round twelve steps, clockwise, each man raising his right hand (and with it his partner's left hand) above his head, and inclining his body slightly to his left. Releasing hands, men turn their partners half-way round, turn their contraries half-way round, rejoin their partners, cross hands and dance round with them counter-clockwise to places.

First and third couples hands-four.

First and third couples Do-si-do-and-promenade-home.

Second and fourth couples hands-four.

Second and fourth couples Do-si-do-and-promenade-home.

FIGURE I

HANDS-FOUR

First and second couples hands-four.

First and third couples hands-four.

First and fourth couples hands-four.

First and fourth couples Do-si-do-and-promenade-home.

FIGURE 2

HANDS-THREE

First man, moving toward the centre, turns his partner with the left hand.

26

First man goes hands-three with the second couple.

First man turns his partner with the left hand.

First man goes hands-three with the third couple; while first woman does the same with the second couple.

First man turns his partner with the left hand.

First man goes hands-three with the fourth couple; while first woman does the same with the third couple.

First man turns his partner with the left hand.

First and fourth couples hands-four.

First and fourth couples Do-si-do-and-promenade-home.

FIGURE 3

SHOOT THE OWL

First man, moving toward the centre, turns his partner with the left hand.

First man goes hands-three with the second couple half-way round and, facing centre, "pops under" the arch made by the second couple, second man and second woman resuming their proper places.

First man turns his partner with the left hand.

First man goes hands-three with the third couple and "pops under" as before; while first woman does the same with the second couple.

First man turns his partner with the left hand.

First man goes hands-three with the fourth couple, "popping under" as before; while the first woman does the same with the third couple.

First man turns his partner with the left hand.

First and fourth couple hands-four.

First and fourth couples Do-si-do-and-promenade-home.

FIGURE 4

CHASE THE SQUIRREL

First man and first woman, joining inside hands, move (the man behind the woman) between second man and second woman, turn to their left and pass, counter-clockwise, round the second woman; while the second woman moves forward four steps and falls back four steps to her place.

Breaking away from her partner, first woman passes between second man and second woman, and moves round a small circle, clockwise, the second man following her round to his place; while the first man executes a *pas seul*.

First man and first woman turn.

First man and first woman go hands-four with the second couple.

The first couple repeats all these movements with the third couple.

The first couple does the same with the fourth couple.

The first and fourth couples Do-si-do-and-promenade-home.

FIGURE 5

The Wild Goose-Chase

First man, taking his partner's left hand in his right and leading her behind him, passes between second man and second woman, turns to his left and moves, counter-clockwise, round second woman.

First man, still leading his partner behind him, moves in front of, and a step or two beyond, second man, casts back, making a half-turn to his right, passes between second man and second woman, turns to his right, clock-wise, round second man, and then goes hands-four with the second couple; while the second man, as the first couple passes by him, breaks away, moves clockwise round his partner to his place, timing his movement so that he shall reach his station just as the four-ring is being formed.

Releasing his left hand, first man breaks away from second woman and, followed by his partner and the second couple, passes between third man and third woman and repeats the same movements with the third couple that he had previously done with the second (the third man doing as the second man did), concluding with hands-six with the third couple.

Releasing his left hand, first man breaks away from third woman and, followed by his partner, second and third couples, passes between fourth man and fourth woman and once again repeats the same movements, concluding with hands-eight with the fourth couple.

Upon the conclusion of the hands-eight, the first man, releasing his left hand, breaks away from the fourth woman, casts back, making a half-turn to his left, and, leading the other seven dancers behind him, moves round in a circle (back to centre), counter-clockwise to his place.

First man casts back, making a half-turn to his right, and leads the other dancers round in a circle (faces to centre), clockwise, to places.

During the performance of this Figure each dancer must be careful to follow exactly in the track of the dancer in front.

FIGURE 6

Box the Gnat

First man turns his partner half-way round with the right hand and once round with the left hand.

First man turns right and left in like manner with second woman; while his partner does the same with second man.

First man turns his partner half-way round with the right hand and once round with the left hand.

First man turns right and left in like manner with third woman; while his partner does the same with third man.

First man turns his partner half-way round with the right hand and once round with the left hand.

First man turns right and left in like manner with fourth woman; while his partner does the same with fourth man.

First and fourth couples hands-four.

First and fourth couples Do-si-do-and-promenade-home.

FIGURE 7

GOING DOWN TOWN

The first couple, facing the opposite (*i.e.*, the third) couple, moves forward four steps.

The first couple falls back four steps to places; while the third couple moves forward four steps.

The third couple falls back four steps to places; while the first couple moves forward and passes between third man and third woman.

First man casts off to his left behind the fourth couple to his place; while first woman casts off to her right behind the second couple to her place.

All the men turn their partners half-way round, turn their contraries half-way round and, staying with their contraries, cross hands and dance once round with them counter-clockwise.

The above movements are now repeated three times, first man and fourth woman facing third man and second woman in the first repetition; first man and third woman facing third man and first woman in the second; and first man and second woman facing third man and fourth woman in the third. The men are now in their own places.

FIGURE 8

BIRD IN THE CAGE

First man leads his partner forward toward second couple and goes hands-three with second couple round her.

First man, breaking with second woman, goes hands-five with second and third couples round his partner.

First man, breaking with third woman, goes hands-seven with second, third, and fourth couples round his partner, and then, immediately the ring is formed, changes places with his partner, stands in the centre facing his station and executes a *pas seul* while the others dance round him to places.

The first woman should edge toward the centre as the successive rings are formed around her, so that when the seven-ring is made she shall be in the centre of the Set.

FIGURE 9

TREAT 'EM ALL RIGHT

First man turns his partner once round with the left hand, and then turns second woman in like manner.

First man turns his partner with the left hand and then third woman in like manner.

First man turns his partner with the left hand and then fourth woman in like manner.

First man turns his partner with the left hand, then fourth woman with the left hand, third woman with the right hand, second woman with the left hand and, finally, his partner with the right hand.

FIGURE 10

RIGHTS AND LEFTS

Circular-hey,* handing, once round, partners facing.

The circular-hey is then repeated, the dancers, instead of handing alternately with right and left, arming once round alternately with right and left arms.

* See *The Country Dance Book*, Part IV., p. 22.

This latter evolution is known as The Lock Chain Swing.

FIGURE II

THE CALIFORNIA SHOW BASKET*

First and second couples hands-across once round clockwise, men joining both hands, and women joining both hands, the men's hands being above the women's.

The men, raising their hands over the heads of the women and lowering them to waist-level, enclose the women and all four go once round clockwise.

The women lift their hands over the heads of the men and rest them on the men's shoulders; while the men raise their hands to the level of the women's necks. In this position all move round once clockwise.

First man turns second woman into her place; while first woman turns second man into his place.

The first couple repeats these movements with the third couple.

The first couple repeats these movements with the fourth couple.

It is suggested that the second circuit (i.e., when the men are enclosing the women) should be executed counter-clockwise.

FIGURE 12

FIGURE EIGHT

The first couple join inside hands and move toward the second couple.

First woman, passing in front of her partner, moves counter-clockwise round second woman; while first man moves clockwise round second man.

First man turns his partner with the right hand.

* Sometimes called The Old Shuck Basket.

Passing in front of his partner, first man moves counter-clockwise round second woman; while first woman moves clockwise round second man.

First man turns his partner with the left hand.

First and second couples hands-four.

The first couple repeats the same movements with the third couple.

The first couple repeats the same movement with the fourth couple.

First and fourth couples Do-si-do-and-promenade-home.

FIGURE 13

LADIES IN THE CENTRE

Men turn their partners three-quarters round and place them back-to-back in the centre of the Set.

The men dance once-and-a-quarter round the women, counter-clockwise, and then turn the women opposite to them, *i.e.*, the women standing on the left of their partners.

The men again dance once-and-a-quarter round the women, counter-clockwise, and then turn each the woman next on the left, cross hands, and dance once round with her counter-clockwise.

The men turn the women they have just danced with and place them back-to-back in the centre of the Set.

The men dance once-and-a-quarter round the women, counter-clockwise, and turn each the woman on the left of the one they have just turned into the centre.

The men dance once-and-a-quarter round the women, counter-clockwise, and then turn their partners, this turn initiating the Grand Promenade, which begins the following Part.

This Figure is sometimes repeated, the women putting the men into the centre, etc.

C

FIGURE 14

Wind up the Ball Yarn*

All join inside hands except first man and fourth woman. Fourth man and fourth woman make an arch.

First man, followed by his partner, second and third couples, passes under the arch, turns to his right and moves round in a circle clockwise. As the third woman passes under the arch, the fourth man turns on his axis three-quarters round, clockwise, and places his right hand over his left shoulder. The fourth man is now said to be "locked."

Fourth man and third woman now make an arch under which the first man passes, followed by his partner, second couple, and third man, turning to his right as before. This locks the third woman.

This circular movement is repeated until the first woman is locked.

Fourth woman places her right hand over her left shoulder; while first man makes a whole turn clockwise; places his right hand over his left shoulder and clasps the fourth woman's right hand with his left.

All dance round, clockwise, to places.

The path which the first man traces after passing under each arch should be as nearly as possible a circle.

The dancers, as they are locked, should move in toward the centre, so that when the first man links up with the fourth woman the eight dancers may be in a circle.

Unwind the Ball Yarn

At the conclusion of the last repetition of the preceding Figure (led by fourth man), the dancers may, if they please, unwind themselves, as follows:—

* Sometimes known as Killiecrankie or The Grapevine Twist, or Winding up the Maple Leaf.

Fourth man, releasing his left hand, raises his right arm, unwinds himself by making a whole turn clockwise, then passes under an arch made by fourth woman and first man, turns to his right, and moves round in a circle, clockwise, as in the preceding movement, unlocking fourth woman.

Fourth man, followed by his partner, passes under an arch made by first man and first woman, turns to his right as before and unlocks first man.

These movements are repeated until all the dancers are unlocked.

Hands-eight to places.

TUCKER

At the conclusion of the Running Set it is customary to dance Tucker, a variant of the well-known children's singing game, The Jolly Miller, as follows:

A fifth man joins the dancers and stands in the centre of the Set. He is called Tucker.

Hands-eight once round.

Men turn their partners half-way round, their contraries half-way round, move forward, rejoin their partners, cross hands with them and dance round counter-clockwise. During the turning movements—*i.e.*, when the dancers are for the moment disengaged—Tucker endeavours to dispossess one of the men of his partner and capture her for himself. If he is successful, the man, whose partner has been stolen, takes his place in the centre and becomes Tucker in the next round.

While the dancers are circling round him, Tucker should dance a hoe-down, or perform any fancy steps that he pleases.

NOTATION

———

As already explained, the order in which the Figures are performed is determined by the Caller. In this Notation the Figures are presented in the order in which they happened to be danced at Hyden.

INTRODUCTION (p. 26)

PART 1

Grand Promenade (p. 26).
Fig. 1, HANDS-FOUR (p. 26), led by first couple.
Little Promenade (p. 26).
Fig. 1, led by second couple.*
Little Promenade.
Fig. 1, led by third couple.*
Little Promenade.
Fig. 1, led by fourth couple.*

PART 2

Grand Promenade.
Fig. 2, HANDS-THREE (p. 26), led by first couple.
Little Promenade.
Fig. 2, led by second couple.
Little Promenade.
Fig. 2, led by third couple.
Little Promenade.
Fig. 2, led by fourth couple.

*In this, and in all similar cases, it must be understood that the leading couple always begins the Figure by engaging the next couple on the right, that is, moving round counter-clockwise.

PART 3

Grand Promenade.
Fig. 3, SHOOT THE OWL (p. 27), led by first couple.
Little Promenade.
Fig. 3, led by second couple.
Little Promenade.
Fig. 3, led by third couple.
Little Promenade.
Fig. 3, led by fourth couple.

PART 4

Grand Promenade.
Fig. 4, CHASE THE SQUIRREL (p. 27), led by first couple
Little Promenade.
Fig. 4, led by second couple.
Little Promenade.
Fig. 4, led by third couple.
Little Promenade.
Fig. 4, led by fourth couple.

PART 5

Grand Promenade.
Fig. 5, THE WILD GOOSE-CHASE (p. 28), led by first
couple.
Little Promenade.
Fig. 5, led by second couple.
Little Promenade.
Fig. 5, led by third couple.
Little Promenade.
Fig. 5, led by fourth couple.

Part 6

Grand Promenade.
Fig. 6, BOX THE GNAT (p. 29), led by first couple.
Little Promenade.
Fig. 6, led by second couple.
Little Promenade.
Fig. 6, led by third couple.
Little Promenade.
Fig. 6, led by fourth couple.

Part 7

Grand Promenade.
Fig. 7, GOING DOWN TOWN (p. 30), led by first couple.
Fig. 7, led by second couple.
Fig. 7, led by third couple.
Fig. 7, led by fourth couple.

> *The construction of this Figure being somewhat irregular, the Little Promenade, which ordinarily separates the repetitions of the Figure, is incorporated in the Figure itself and does not, therefore, appear in the above Notation. The concluding movement of the last repetition of the Figure, led by fourth man, becomes the initial movement of the Grand Promenade which begins the next Part.*

Part 8

Grand Promenade.
Fig. 8, BIRD IN THE CAGE (p. 30), led by first couple.
Little Promenade.
Fig. 8, led by second couple.
Little Promenade.
Fig. 8, led by third couple.
Little Promenade.
Fig. 8, led by fourth couple.

PART 9

Grand Promenade.
Fig. 9, TREAT 'EM ALL RIGHT (p. 31), led by first couple.
Little Promenade.
Fig. 9, led by second couple.
Little Promenade.
Fig. 9, led by third couple.
Little Promenade.
Fig. 9, led by fourth couple.

PART 10

Grand Promenade.
Fig. 10, RIGHTS AND LEFTS (p. 31).

PART 11

Grand Promenade.
Fig. 11, THE CALIFORNIA SHOW BASKET (p. 32), led by first couple.
Little Promenade.
Fig. 11, led by second couple.
Little Promenade.
Fig. 11, led by third couple.
Little Promenade.
Fig. 11, led by fourth couple.

PART 12

Grand Promenade.
Fig. 12, FIGURE EIGHT (p. 32), led by first couple.
Little Promenade.
Fig. 12, led by second couple.
Little Promenade.
Fig. 12, led by third couple.
Little Promenade.
Fig. 12, led by fourth couple.

PART 13

Grand Promenade.
Fig. 13, LADIES IN THE CENTRE (p. 33).

PART 14

Grand Promenade.
Fig. 14, WIND UP THE BALL YARN (p. 34), led by first
man.
Little Promenade.
Fig. 14, led by second man.
Little Promenade.
Fig. 14, led by third man.
Little Promenade.
Fig. 14, led by fourth man.
UNWIND THE BALL YARN (p. 34).

TUCKER (p. 35)

APPENDIX A.

ADDITIONAL FIGURES

FIGURE 15

THE WALTZ-SWING

*As danced at Quicksand (Breathitt Co., Ky.) and ex-
plained by Mr. Sewell Williams.*

First man, moving toward the centre, turns his partner
with the left hand.

First man goes hands-three with the second couple.

First man turns his partner with the left hand.

First man goes hands-three with the third couple;
while first woman does the same with the second couple.

The three-rings continue revolving, while the rings
themselves move round each other, each ring making
one complete circuit clockwise.

First man turns his partner with the left hand.

First man goes hands-three with the fourth couple;
while first woman goes hands-three with the third couple.

The three-rings continue to revolve while the rings
themselves move round each other, clockwise, each ring
making one complete circuit.

First and fourth couples hands-four.

First and fourth couples Do-si-do-and-promenade-home.

FIGURE 16

Cutting Off Three, Two, and One

As danced at Quicksand (Breathitt Co., Ky.) and explained by Mr. Sewell Williams.

The first couple moves forward four steps toward the third couple and falls back four steps to places.

First man and first woman again move forward, pass between third man and third woman ("cutting off three") and cast off to places, the man to his left behind the fourth couple, the woman to her right behind the second couple.

All partners turn.

The first couple moves forward and back toward the third couple as before.

First man passes between third woman and fourth man; while first woman passes between second woman and third man ("cutting off two"); whereupon, both cast off to places, the first man to his left, the first woman to her right.

All partners turn.

The first couple moves forward and back toward the third couple as before.

First man passes between fourth man and fourth woman; while first woman passes between second man and second woman ("cutting off one"); whereupon, both cast off to places, first man to his left, first woman to her right.

All partners turn.

FIGURE 17

Hands-Across

As danced at Quicksand (Breathitt Co., Ky.) and explained by Mr. Sewell Williams.

All partners turn.

First and second couples right-hands-across (eight steps).

First and second couples left-hands-across (eight steps).

First and second couples Do-si-do.

All partners turn.

First and third couples right- and left-hands-across and Do-si-do, as before.

All partners turn.

First and fourth couples right- and left-hands-across, as before.

First and fourth couples Do-si-do-and-promenade-home.

APPENDIX B.

VARIANTS

The Grand Promenade

As danced at Quicksand (Breathitt Co., Ky.) and explained by Mr. Sewell Williams.

Hands-eight, once round, clockwise to places.

Men turn their partners half-way round with the right hand, turn their contraries half-way round with the left hand, rejoin their partners, cross hands and dance round with them, counter-clockwise, to places.

This is the only Promenade used at Quicksand and is performed between the repetitions of the Figures as well as at the beginning of each Part.

The Introduction

As danced at Quicksand (Breathitt Co., Ky.) and explained by Mr. Sewell Williams.

Grand Promenade (Quicksand variant; see above).

First and third couples move forward a double and fall back a double to places.

First and third couples move forward eight steps, cross over, and change places, opposites passing by the right.

First and third couples move forward a double, fall back a double, and cross over to places.

Second and fourth couples move forward a double, fall back a double, cross over, and change places.

Second and fourth couples move forward a double, fall back a double, and cross over to places.

FIGURE 5

THE WILD GOOSE-CHASE

As danced at Quicksand (Breathitt Co., Ky.) and explained by Mr. Sewell Williams.

This is danced in the same way as the Hyden variant given in the text with the following additional movements:

(1) First man turns his partner at the beginning, *i.e.,* before leading her between second man and second woman.

(2) After the hands-four, which concludes the movement between first and second couples, these two couples do the Do-si-do.

(3) After the hands-six, which concludes the movement between first, second, and third couples, first, second, and third men turn their partners and then turn their contraries, as in the Promenade, before they engage the fourth couple.

FIGURE 6

BOX THE GNAT

As danced at Quicksand (Breathitt Co., Ky.) and explained by Mr. Sewell Williams.

First man and first woman arm-right and face second couple.

First man arms-left with second woman; while first woman arms-left with second man.

First man arms-right with his partner.

First man arms-left with third woman; while first woman arms-left with third man.

First man arms-right with his partner.

First man arms-left with fourth woman; while first woman arms-left with fourth man.

As danced at Hindman (Knott Co., Ky.).

This is the same as the Hyden version given in the text, except that in the left-hand turn the man turns completely round on his own axis, clockwise.

FIGURE 8

BIRD IN THE CAGE

As danced at Quicksand (Breathitt Co., Ky.) and explained by Mr. Sewell Williams.

First man turns his partner and swings her toward second man and second woman.

First man goes hands-three with the second couple round first woman.

First man changes places with first woman, who goes hands-three with second couple round him.

First man turns his partner.

First and second couples Do-si-do.

First man goes hands-five with second and third couples round first woman.

First woman changes places with her partner and goes hands-five with second and third couples round him.

First man turns his partner.

First man goes hands-seven with second, third, and fourth couples round first woman.

First woman changes places with her partner and goes hands-seven with second, third, and fourth couples round him.

First man turns his partner.

FIGURE 17

HANDS-ACROSS

As danced at Hyden (Leslie Co., Ky.) and explained by Miss Dickson.

First and second couples right-hands-across.

First and second couples left-hands-across.

First man turns second woman; while second man turns first woman.

First and second couples hands-four.

First and third couples do likewise.

First and fourth couples do likewise.

First and fourth couples Do-si-do-and-promenade· home.

METHOD OF PROGRESSION

As danced at Quicksand (Breathitt Co., Ky.) and explained by Mr. Sewell Williams,

In those Figures in which the leading couple engages the other couples in turn, it was customary, when the leading couple was dancing with the last couple, for the other two couples simultaneously to perform the same movements.

Again, in those Figures which begin with the leading man turning his partner, it was usual for the other three men to turn their partners also.

These variants, Mr. Sewell explained, were performed only when the Set consisted of experienced dancers who were accustomed to dance together.

APPENDIX C.

DIRECTIONS USED BY THE "CALLER" AT PINE MOUNTAIN (HARLAN CO., KY.)

Join hands, circle left.
Home swing, one and all.
First gent, swing off four.
Last four, Ladies, Do-si,
    Gents, low g,
    Swing 'em right,
    Swing 'em left,
    Keep 'em when you find 'em
    And don't turn 'em loose,
    Come your partner, promenade.
Home swing,
Balance eight and keep 'em straight.

Partners on the left and swing three,
Partners follow, three by six.
Ladies Do-si,
Home swing,
Balance eight.

Partner on the left and shoot the owl,
Partner follow,
Do-si, ladies, etc.,
Home swing and balance eight.

Lady round the lady and the gent also,
Lady round the gent and the gent don't go,

Swing her around,
Four on the square over here,
Do-si, ladies, etc.,
Home swing and balance eight.

Bird in the cage and three hands round,
Bird in the cage and five hands round, etc.,
Bird hops out and crow hops in.
Everybody swing,
Balance eight.

First couple lead out and box those gnats,
Cheat 'em if you can,
Four on the corner, etc.

First gent lead out and chase the squirrel,
Break to the left and round the lady,
Back to the right and round the gent,
Four on this square over here,
Ladies Do-si.

Home swing,
Promenade inside the ring.
Swing your partner,
Cast off three,
Swing your partner,
Cast off two, etc.,
Everybody swing, balance eight.

Ladies in the centre and back-to-back,
While the gents go galloping round,
Come your partners, swing,
Pass your partners once,
Pass your partners twice,
Pass your partners three,
Come your partner, promenade,
Home swing,
Gents in the centre, etc.

D

California show-basket.
Ladies in the centre and right-hands-across half-way
　round,
Left-hands-across and back.
Ladies join hands (on inside circle),
Gents join hands outside,
Come your partner, lock circles.
Circle left (locked) to home,
Home swing, one and all,
Balance eight, everybody swing.

Join hands, circle left.
First gent lead out a wild goose-chase,
Break to the left and round the lady,
Break to the right around the gent,
Four hands up and going again,
Break to the left, etc.,
Six hands up and going again. etc.,
Eight hands up and going again, circle left,
Break to the left in a wild goose-chase,
Break to the right and going again,
Come your places, home swing,
Balance eight,
Join hands, circle left.

Killiecrankie is my song,
I sing and dance it all along,
From my elbow to my wrist
Heavy turn and double twist.
How much further can I go
From my elbow to my toe?
Sheepskin, a sharpskin,
Forty twenty yaller girls
Dancing on sheepskin.
　　　　　First gent goes under arm of fourth,
　　　　　Gent circle and then under third, etc.,
　　　　　　until all are unlocked,

    Circle left and either unwind or home **swing,**
    Balance eight.

Tucker.
Tucker dance,
Circle left, everybody swing,
Give old Tucker one more show,
Let's quit,
      or
Promenade your partner to her seat
And choose your partner for the next Set.

IOHANNIS PLAYFORD

JOHN PLAYFORD.
1623 1686.

THE

COUNTRY DANCE BOOK

PART VI.

CONTAINING

FIFTY-TWO COUNTRY DANCES

FROM

THE ENGLISH DANCING MASTER

(1650—1728)

DESCRIBED BY

CECIL J. SHARP.

LONDON : NOVELLO AND COMPANY, LIMITED.

NEW YORK : THE H. W. GRAY CO., SOLE AGENTS FOR THE U.S.A.

CONTENTS.

Kettle Drum   A round Dance for eight

Meete all, and back ∴   That   We. meete, giving their right hands, men meete , giving their right hands , then
againe ∴   turne every man his owne Wo. by the right hand , then men the left hands , We.
                       their left hands, then turne every Wo. her owne man by the left hand ∴

Sides all, back againe ∴   That   The 2. Cu. meete and fall back, then the next Cu. meete, and take each others Wo.
againe ∴   by the right hand , and fall into the Co. places, then the other Cu. meete and fall
                     back, and the first Cu. the like, then leade in, taking the We. by the right hand, and
                     cast off to your places ∴

Armes all ∴   That again ∴   All joyne both hands with your We. swing with your hands all inward , then
                         breake off your hands inward, then turn back to back, and kisse the Co. Wo. twice,
                         then swing with the Co. We. all outwards ; then breake off your hands outwards,
                         then turne kissing every one his owne Wo. turne and so end ∴

N

From *The English Dancing Master* (1st Ed. 1650)

INTRODUCTION.

THIS book contains a further instalment of fifty-two dances selected from "The English Dancing Master"; eighteen from the first four editions (1650-70), three from the 7th edition (1686), one from the 8th (1690), seven from the 10th (1698), eleven from the 11th (1701), nine from the 12th (1703), and the remaining three from the 14th (1709). These dances, with those already published in Parts 2, 3, and 4 of this Series, make a total of 159, *i.e.*, 21 Rounds; 6 Square-eights; 11 For-four; 21 Longways-for-six; 15 Longways-for-eight; and 85 Longways for as many as will.

Of the 24 Rounds, which are all that "The English Dancing Master" and subsequent editions contain, we have now accounted for all but three—" The Chirping of the Nightingale," "Kemp's Jig," and "Kettle Drum." The first two present no difficulties in the way of interpretation, and have been omitted only because they are not of sufficient interest to warrant printing. "Kettle Drum," however, has a splendid tune (set to "Peppers Black" in the present volume) and movements which would apparently be interesting enough could they be deciphered, but this, despite repeated attempts, I have so far been unable to do. In the hope, however, that some of my readers may be more ingenious, and partly, I admit, in self-justification, a facsimile of Playford's notation of the dance is here reproduced.

The dances For-four and the Square-eights have proved more amenable, and every one of the dances of these two types that the Playford books contain has now been deciphered and printed. I would that there were more of them.

Of the Longways-for-six in " The Dancing Master " all but
seven have now been published, and of the Longways-for-
eight all but ten. A few of the seventeen dances thus omitted
were rejected because their interpretation was uncertain, and
the remainder because they were not sufficiently interesting
to merit publication.

The seventy-four dances above enumerated represent, I
regret to say, all the older forms of the Country Dance that it
seems possible to extract from " The English Dancing
Master," and, moreover, all that we shall ever possess ; for,
as already explained, this type of dance gradually fell into
disuse during the latter years of the 17th century, and
disappeared altogether with the opening years of the following
century. All that now remains, therefore, to complete our
investigations is to examine more closely than we have yet
done the editions subsequent to the 14th (1709), and select
therefrom those Progressive dances that may seem worthy of
preservation.

In the Introduction to my first book of Playford dances,
published in 1911, I gave as careful and detailed a description
as I was at that time able to give, of these 17th century
dances, of the way in which they were noted in " The English
Dancing Master," and, in general terms, of the problems to
be solved in their interpretation. I have not since
returned to this subject, having been content to publish, in
Parts 3 and 4 of this series, the results of further researches
without comment. The reader, however, is entitled, and will
probably wish, to know how far further investigations and a
closer acquaintance with the Playford volumes have affected
the opinions I then expressed. This claim I will now meet ;
the more readily because in preparing the second and third
selections of dances I was assisted by George Butterworth,
who brought a keen and unusually ingenious mind to bear
upon the subject, and succeeded in elucidating many

troublesome points that had hitherto baffled me; and in compiling the present volume, although unhappily deprived of his valuable and kindly help, I have been aided by Miss Maud Karpeles, whose name should, and but for her refusal to allow it, would have appeared upon the title-page. Any views that I have now to express are, therefore, those of my two collaborators as much as my own.

The chief difficulties to be resolved in deciphering these dances have been : (1) to interpret the language of the Playford notations ; (2) to determine the steps that were used in the 17th century Country Dance, a question upon which Playford and other contemporary authorities are silent ; and (3) to capture the spirit and style of the dance.

Continued research has thrown little or no additional light on either of the last two questions. Concerning the steps, however, there is this to be said, that those which I originally propounded have been tested in the last ten years in a very practical way, and in the result have been found to be serviceable and to satisfy the needs of the dance. Even if, therefore, they are not historically accurate—as in the main I still believe them to be—they at any rate serve their purpose. And this, as later on I shall have occasion to point out, is the chief, if not the only, function of the steps in a dance which, like the one in question, depends almost wholly for its expressiveness upon figure-movements.

Nor do I think that we can have gone very far astray in our restoration of the dance so far as its character and spirit are concerned. The words of " a lady of distinction," already quoted, seem to me to tell us all that we need to know, viz., that " The characteristic of an English Country Dance is that of gay simplicity. The steps should be few and easy, and the corresponding motions of the arms and body unaffected, modest, and graceful." Confirmation of this estimate is, moreover, implicit in the many references to the dance in contemporary writings both before and after 1650, one and all of which testify to the unsophisticated, jolly character of the dance and to the pleasant contrast which in this respect it afforded to the ceremonial dances of the Court. But stronger still than any documentary support is the evidence of the dance itself—the spirit and character which pervade its every movement and are reflected in every phrase of the accompanying music.

In regard, then, to these two important points I think it may fairly be claimed that the dance has not been unfaithfully presented. Where we may and no doubt have failed, in greater or less degree, is in our interpretation of the movements and figures. The loose, unscientific, happy-go-lucky way in which the descriptions of the dances are often worded ; the frequent use of undefined technical terms and expressions that became obsolete during the period covered by the Playford volumes ; the typographical errors which disfigure so many of the pages—the inaccurate punctuation, the omission of important words, sometimes of whole sentences — these make a really accurate, scientifically exact, transcription humanly unattainable. Nevertheless, by exercising reasonable care, by confining the published dances to those least liable to miscon-struction, by noting and allowing for the kind of error to which experience shows that the Playford editors and compositors were most prone, it has been feasible to reduce to comparatively small proportions, and in some cases entirely to eliminate, the element of speculation.

We have now, I think, arrived at the meaning of all the technical terms used in the notations, with one exception—the Side. Further evidence which has come to light with respect to this very troublesome figure seems to throw doubt upon the accuracy of the half-turn in each portion of the figure, in the form in which I reconstructed it. Now if,

Mundesse   Round for fix

face p. 11]

Hands and two D. round, fet and turne S. —
That againe ∴

Firft man fet and turne S. ∸
His Wo. as much ∴

Firft man honor
to his Wo. 2. as
much, 3. as much.
All embrace.

Turne your
own — turn
Co. ∴

Firft man lead his Wo. 2. D. forwards and
back ∴ Lead forwards again, go each between
the 2. Cu. and come back againe in the fame —

Firft Wo. fet and turne S. —
To the Co. man — The man
as much ∴

Honor to her next
man, honor to the
Co. Wo. 3. honor.
Imbrace all.

As before ∴

Firft Wo. lead the Co. man as before ∴

Second man fet and turne S.
to his own Wo. ∴ The Wo.
as much ∴

honor to her next
man, firft honor,
Imbrace all your
We.

As before ∴

Lead in, every man doing as the firft did.

From *The English Dancing Master* (1st Ed. 1650).

instead of turning, the dancers were to " fall back to places " along their own tracks, the Side would then be identical with the Morris figure of Half-hands, or Half-gip. And this, I suspect, may prove to be the correct interpretation ; but until it is supported by far more definite and conclusive evidence than we at present have, it would, I think, be unwise to make any alteration in the figure as it is now executed.

I wish it were possible to lay bare our method fully and to explain in detail the way in which we have dealt with the many difficulties above referred to, but this would be an impracticably long task and occupy more space than can be spared. One or two illustrations, however, may perhaps be allowed.

One constant source of trouble arises from the apparent inability of the recorders of some of the notations to describe accurately in technical language the changes in the successive repetitions of a figure-sequence. " Mundesse," a facsimile of which is here reproduced, may be taken, and not unfairly I think, to illustrate the perplexities which proceed from this cause.

Playford's notation of this dance looks at first sight very puzzling ; but when the plan upon which the dance is constructed is realised, it is not difficult to divine what the writer intended but was unable to express. It is merely a matter of the order in which the honours are paid, and this order will automatically change as the figure moves round the circle, one place in each successive repetition. Our interpretation (*see* p. 60), which is based on this supposition is, I believe, substantially correct.

The second figure (B music) of the first Part of " Newcastle " affords another illustration of a like confusion, as the reader will see if he will refer to the reproduction of the dance given in Part 2 (*see* p. 77). The second half of this figure was intended no doubt to be complementary to

and symmetrical with the first ; but it is not so noted.   The
last sentence should of course read: " Armes againe with
your owne by the left, and We. right hands in, men goe
about them towards the right to your places." *   A figure very
similar to this occurs in the second Part of " Chelsea Reach "
(Part 3, p. 36), but here a general direction only is given
for the second half of the figure, the dancers being left to
work out the technique for themselves—a much safer plan.

In a few special cases I have felt justified in making minor
technical changes when by so doing the execution of a difficult
passage was made easier or less awkward.   In the first figure
of the third Part of " Step Stately " (Part 4, p. 59), for
instance, the movement is very greatly improved by making
the two files fall back before moving forward, instead of
reversing these movements, as the dancers are directed to do
in the original text.

In the Progressive dances of the later editions the chief
trouble has been to adjust the movements to the several
sections of the music.   In the earlier editions the apportion-
ment of music to figure is usually indicated in the notations,
but for some unexplained reason this helpful plan was dis-
continued in the later volumes.   This has added very
considerably to our troubles, especially when, as is not
infrequent, no directions are given concerning the number
of repetitions, if any, of the several sections of the music.
Here again an illustration may be helpful.   In " Apley
House " (*see* p. 120), for instance, the music consists of three
four-bar sections, but with no directions about repeats, as the
following transcription of the notation will show :—

> " The two men take hands and fall back, and
> turn single ;   the women do the same: Hands-
> across half-round, and turn single.   The second

---

* The double figure in the third Part of this dance is correctly noted—"turn" at
the end of the first line being obviously a misprint for "turne S."

> couple being in the first place, cast off, and the other couple follow and lead up a-breast; the first couple cross over into the second couple's place, the second couple lead up and cross over into their own places."

In this case I believe our solution is probably right, but I am aware that there is room for differences of opinion. Incidentally, our notation of this dance will serve to give a general idea of the way in which we have expanded the original text and translated it into present-day technical language.

We have now perhaps said enough to indicate the general lines we have followed in our attempt to reconstruct the dances. Those who wish for further information can obtain it by consulting the original texts and comparing them with our translations.

It is impossible to examine the dances of the later editions without being impressed by the beauty of a large number of the tunes they contain. These, with few exceptions, are frankly composed, sophisticated tunes, and it would be interesting to know by whom they were written or from what sources they were derived. The volumes themselves give us no information whatever about their origin. Some, I imagine, may have been definitely composed for the Country Dance, but I suspect the majority were contemporary airs pressed into the service of the dance by the Playford editors. " The Siege of Limerick " (" Country Dance Tunes," Set 10) is the tune of one of Purcell's songs, " O how happy's he," and I cannot resist a suspicion that the same master-hand was responsible also for several of the other triple-time hornpipe airs, *e.g.*, " Dick's Maggot," " Mr. Isaac's Maggot," " The Hare's Maggot," etc. Two of the airs to the dances in this volume were later on used in " The Beggar's Opera "— " Of Noble Race was Shinkin " (set to " Nowill Hills ") and " Greenwich Park."

Whatever their origin, the beauty of these airs is incontestable, and if we may believe that the Country Dance attracted the attention of the best musicians of the day, and induced them to give of their best to its service, this would be further testimony, were it needed, of the important place which the National dance held in the social life of that period.

C. J. S.

Hampstead,
March, 1922.

THE DANCE.

THE ROOM.

THE following diagram is a ground plan of the room in which the dances are supposed to take place:—

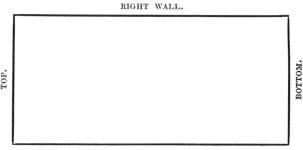

A diagram, showing the initial disposition of the dancers, is printed at the head of the notation of each dance, and placed so that its four sides correspond with the four sides of the room as depicted in the above plan. That is, the upper and lower sides of the diagram represent, respectively, the right and left walls of the room; its left and right sides the top and bottom.

In Playford's time, the top of the room was called *the Presence*, alluding to the dais upon which the spectators were seated. The expression *facing the Presence* means, therefore, facing up, *i.e.*, toward the top of the room; while *back to the Presence* means facing down, toward the bottom of the room.

TECHNICAL TERMS AND SYMBOLS.

O = man ; ☐ = woman.

r. = a step taken with the right foot ; l. = a step taken with the left foot.

h.r. = a hop on to the right foot ; l.r. = a hop on to the left foot.

The *Set* or the *General Set* is the area occupied or enclosed by the dancers in any given dance-formation.

A *Longways dance* is one in which the performers take partners and stand in two parallel lines, the men on one side opposite and facing their partners on the other, those on the men's side facing the right wall, those on the women's side the left wall.

The disposition of the dancers in a longways dance is said to be *proper* when the men and women are on their own sides; and *improper* when the men are on the women's side or the women on the men's.

A *Progressive dance* consists of the repetition for an indefinite number of times of a series of movements, called the *Complete Figure*, each repetition being performed by the dancers in changed positions. The performance of each Complete Figure is called a *Round*.

A *Progressive movement* or *figure* is one the performance of which leaves the dancers relatively in different positions.

A *neutral* dancer is one who, in a progressive dance, is passive during the performance of a Round.

In dances or figures in which two couples only are engaged, the terms *contrary woman* and *contrary man* are used to denote the woman or man other than the partner.

When two dancers standing side by side are directed to *take hands* they are to join inside hands : that is, the right hand of one with the left hand of the other, if the two face the same way ; and right hands or left hands, if they face in opposite directions. When they are directed to take, or give, right or left hands, they are to join right with right, or left with left.

To *cross hands* the man takes the right and left hands of the woman with his right and left hands respectively, the right hands being held above the left.

When two dancers face one another and are directed to take *both hands*, they are to join right with left and left with right.

To pass *by the right* is to pass right shoulder to right shoulder; *by the left*, left shoulder to left shoulder.

When two dancers pass each other they should always, unless otherwise directed, pass each other by the right.

When a woman's path crosses that of a man's, the man should allow the woman to pass first and in front of him.

When one dancer is directed to *lead* another, the two join right or left hands according as the second dancer stands on the right or left hand of the leader.

To *cast off* is to turn outward and dance outside the General Set.

To *cast up* or *cast down* is to turn outward and move up or down outside the General Set.

To *fall* is to dance backwards; to *lead*, or *move*, is to dance forwards.

To make a *half-turn* is to turn through half a circle and face in the opposite direction; to make a *whole-turn* is to make a complete revolution.

The terms *clockwise* and *counter-clockwise* are self-explanatory and refer to the direction of circular movements.

PROGRESSIVE DANCES.

THE PROGRESSIVE LONGWAYS DANCE.

There are two methods of progression in a Longways Dance —the *whole-set* and the *minor-set*.

In the *whole-set* dance the progression is effected by the transference in every Round of the top couple from the top to the bottom of the General Set, the rest of the couples moving up one place.

The *minor-set* dance is one in which the Complete Figure in each Round is performed simultaneously by subsidiary sets or groups of two (*duple*) or three (*triple*) adjacent couples.

The effect of every performance of the Complete Figure is to change the positions of the couples in each minor-set. In a duple minor-set dance the two couples change places, in a triple minor-set the two upper couples. This necessitates a rearrangement of the minor-sets in the following Round, and this is effected by each top couple forming a new minor-set with the adjacent couple or couples below. In this way the top couple of each minor-set will move down the Set one place every Round; while the lower couple of the duple minor-set, and the second couple in the triple minor-set, will each move up one place. The position of the third couple in the triple minor-set will be unaffected, but in the following Round it will, as second couple, move up one place. As the dance proceeds, therefore, every couple will move from one end of the Set to the other, the top couples down, the rest up. In a duple minor-set dance each couple on reaching either end of the General Set becomes neutral in the following Round. In a triple minor-set each couple upon reaching the top of the General Set remains neutral during the two following Rounds; and on reaching the bottom for one Round only. It should be added that when the top couple of a triple minor-set dance reaches the last place but one it must, in the succeeding Round, dance the progressive portion of the Complete Figure with the last couple or change places with them.*

---

* For further and more detailed information respecting the Progressive Longways Dance see *The Country Dance Book*, Part I., pp. 17-24.

THE PROGRESSIVE ROUND.

The direction of the progression is normally counter-clockwise—-as in the Running Set—but in some dances, owing to the exigencies of one or other of the movements of the Complete Figure, the couples progress in the reverse direction, clockwise.

In the diagram at the head of the Notation of each dance, the dancers will be numbered in the direction of the progression. The following diagram, for instance, is of a counter-clockwise dance :—

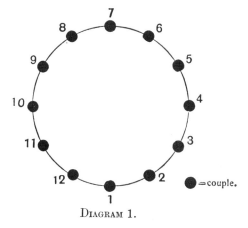

DIAGRAM 1.

The first couple opens the dance by dancing the Complete Figure with the second couple, passing on in the next Round to the third couple and thereafter progressing round the ring. In the third Round the second couple will dance with the third couple and thus become a moving couple, and begin its progression round the ring in the train of the first couple. Similarly every alternate Round a stationary couple will be converted into a moving couple and begin its progression round the ring. By the time the first couple has reached the last couple all the couples (*i.e.*, if the number of couples is even; all but one, if odd) will be engaged, and the General Set will have assumed the form of two concentric half-circles, the inner ring consisting of moving couples, the outer of stationary couples, thus :—

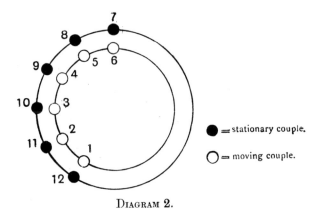

DIAGRAM 2.

In the next Round the first couple having come to the end of the stationary couples will fall back into the outer ring beside the last couple (*i.e.*, its original station), become a stationary couple, and, after one neutral Round, be engaged in turn by the rest of the couples in numerical order; while at the other end of the Set, the 7th couple, after being neutral for one Round, will move into the inner ring, become a moving couple, and progress round the ring engaging the stationary couples in turn.

The procedure should now be clear. At one end of the Set one moving couple will be transferred, every alternate Round, from the inner to the outer ring and become a stationary couple; while at the other end a stationary couple, also every alternate Round, will be transferred from the outer to the inner ring and become a moving couple. The General Set will always consist of a double line of couples occupying one half of the circumference of the original ring, and that half will move slowly round the circle, counter-clockwise, at the rate of one couple every alternate Round.

The dance may end progressively as it began (after the manner of the Progressive Hey), or continue indefinitely with all the couples engaged.

The slow and somewhat tedious opening Rounds of the dance when begun progressively, may be omitted by starting the dance at the point depicted in Diagram 2. In that case it will be possible to accommodate several more couples without enlarging the ring, thus :—

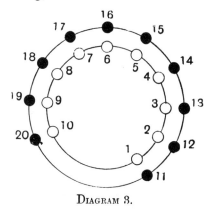

DIAGRAM 3.

So long as the gap or vacant space separating the two ends of the Set is clearly defined and the dancers are careful not to encroach upon it, no confusion need arise. In the above diagram the space allotted to the gap is three couples, and that will probably be found in practice to be sufficient. It should be added that if the Dance is performed in this way, the opening movement, hands-all, will have to be sacrificed. The Sides and Arms, however, can be performed when the dancers are in the double ring.

THE MUSIC.

The several strains of each dance-air will be marked in the music-book and in the notations by means of capital letters, A, B, C, etc.   When a strain is played more than once in a Part it will be marked A1, B1, C1, etc., on its first performance, and A2, B2, C2, A3, B3, etc., in subsequent repetitions.

It will be found that many of the dances in this collection are divided into two or more Parts.   John Essex quaintly but aptly likened these divisions to "the several verses of songs upon the same tune."

In non-progressive dances, the division is made merely for the sake of clearness in description; the Parts are intended to follow on without pause.

When, however, a progressive movement occurs in one or other of the figures of a Part, that Part must be repeated as often as the dancers decree.   The usual practice is to repeat the Part until the leader has returned to his original place.

Progressive figures will be marked as such in the notation; while the Parts in which they occur will be headed " Whole-Set," "Duple Minor-Set," etc., according to the nature of the progression.

MOTION IN THE DANCE.

The Country Dance is pre-eminently a figure dance, depending in the main for its expressiveness upon the weaving of patterned, concerted evolutions rather than upon intricate steps or elaborate body-movements.   That the steps in the Country Dance should be few in number and technically simple is, therefore, natural enough.   For complicated foot-work is obviously incompatible with that free, easy, yet controlled, movement needed in the execution of intricate figures.   In a figure-dance such as we are now considering, the way in which the dancer moves from place to place is obviously of far

PARSON'S FAREWELL.

[Photo. by E. S. Whitney, Huntingdon.

greater importance than the steps, and to this therefore we will first turn our attention. An analysis of the way in which the traditional folk-dancer moves shows that it is based upon two main principles :—

(1.) The weight of the body in motion must always be supported wholly on one foot or the other, and never carried on both feet at the same moment. From this it follows that the transition from step to step, *i.e.*, the transference of the weight from one foot to the other, must always be effected by spring, high enough to raise the body off the ground.

(2.) The motive force, although derived in part from this foot-spring, is chiefly due to the action of gravity, brought into play by the inclination of the body from the vertical. The dancer in motion is always in unstable equilibrium, regulating both the speed and the direction of his movement by varying the poise and balance of his body.* When moving along the straight, for instance, his body will be poised either in front of his feet or behind them, according as his movement is forward or backward ; and laterally when moving along a curved track.*

The function of the legs is to support the body rather than to help to move it forward, the actual motion being set up, regulated, and directed by the sway and balance of the body, as in skating. The body, it should be pointed out, cannot be used in this way, that is to set up and regulate motion, unless it is carried essentially in line from head to foot, without bend at the neck or at the waist, or sag at the knees.

* See photograph on opposite page.

The advantages of this way of moving are obvious. Motion is started and kept up with the least expenditure of muscular energy; it can be regulated, both as to speed and direction, with the greatest ease and nicety; above all, its expressive value is high in that it brings the whole body, and not the legs alone, into play. This last consideration is a weighty one. The strongest argument against " leg-dancing " is not merely that it is ugly, or that it involves superfluous muscular effort, but that the legs, being primarily concerned and almost wholly occupied in supporting and preserving the equilibrium of the body, cannot effectively be employed for expressive or any other purpose.

THE STEPS.

The following general directions apply to the execution of all the steps used in the Country Dance :—

(1.) Country Dance steps always fall on the main divisions of the bar, *i.e.*, on each of the two beats in duple measure ($\frac{2}{2}$ or $\frac{6}{8}$), and of the three beats in triple-measure ($\frac{3}{2}$ or $\frac{9}{8}$). In the case of a compound step, that is, one that comprises more than one movement, the accented movement should fall on the beat.

(2.) The step should fall on the ball of the foot, not on the toe, with the heel off, but close to, the ground.

(3.) The feet should be held straight and parallel, neither turned out nor in at the ankle.

(4.) The legs should never be straddled, but held close together. Nor again should they be extended more than is absolutely necessary; the spring should as far as possible take the place of the stride.

(5.) The jar caused by the impact of the feet on the floor should be absorbed mainly by the ankle-joint, and very little or not at all by the knees. The knees indeed should be bent as little as possible, so little that the legs should appear to be straight, *i.e.*, in one line from hip to ankle.

(6.) All unnecessary movements should be suppressed, *e.g.*, kicking up the heels, fussing with the feet, raising the knees, etc.

THE RUNNING-STEP.

This is the normal Country Dance step. It is an ordinary running-step, executed neatly and lightly, in accordance with the above instructions.

In the notation this will be marked :—

r.s. (running-step).

THE WALKING-STEP.

This is a modified form of the running-step, in which the spring, though present, is scarcely noticeable.

In the notation this will be marked :—

w.s. (walking-step).

SKIPPING-STEP.

This is the usual step-and-hop on alternate feet. The accent is on the step, which must fall, therefore, on the beat. Care should be taken to prevent the skipping-step from degenerating into a double-hop, the two feet taking the ground together, instead of in succession. The hop should fall on the last quarter, or the last third, of the beat according as the latter is simple or compound, thus :—

$$\frac{2}{2}$$ l.   h.l.   r.   h.r. | l.   h.l.   r.   h.r. |

OR

$$\frac{6}{8}$$ r.   h.r.   l.   h.l. | r.   h.r.   l.   h.l. |

In the notation this will be marked :—

sk.s. (skipping-step).

SLIPPING-STEP.

This is a series of springs, made sideways, off alternate feet, the major spring being on to the outside foot, *i.e.*, the left when going to the left and the right when going to the right. Although the legs are thus alternately opening and closing, scissor-fashion, the motion is effected almost wholly by the spring, not the straddle; the legs, therefore, should be separated as little as possible. The free foot should not be allowed to scrape the ground.

The accent falls on the foot on to which the major spring is made, that is, the left or right, according to the direction of motion, thus :—

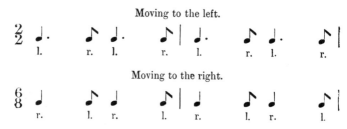

Moving to the left.

Moving to the right.

In the notation this will be marked :—

sl.s. (slipping-step).

THE DOUBLE-HOP.

This is sometimes, though very rarely, used in ring movements as an alternative to the slipping-step. It is a variant of the Slip, in which the feet, instead of taking the ground separately one after the other, alight together a few inches apart.

THE SINGLE.

Playford defines the Single as "two steps, closing the feet." Technically this may be interpreted in the following way: on the first beat of the bar a spring is made, forwards or sideways, on to one foot, say the right; the left foot is then brought up beside it, the weight wholly or in part momentarily supported upon it, and, on the second beat of the bar, transferred to the right foot in position.

This step is subject to various modifications, partly individual, but more often arising from the character of the dance or phrase in which the step occurs. Many dancers, for instance, never allow the foot upon which the initial spring is made (*i.e.*, the right foot in the above description) to leave the ground when the left foot is brought up beside it; but instead, rise on the toes of both feet on the intermediate accent, and then on the second beat sink back on to the ball of the right foot.

THE DOUBLE.

This is defined in *The English Dancing Master* as "four steps forward or backward closing the feet," *i.e.*, four running or walking steps, the last of which is made in position (that is, beside the other foot), the weight being supported either on the one foot or on both feet, according to circumstances.

THE TURN SINGLE.

The dancer makes a whole turn on his axis, clockwise (unless otherwise directed), taking four (in triple measure, three or six) low springing steps off alternate feet, beginning with the right foot. The body must be held erect, and the turn regulated so that the dancer completes the circle and regains his original position on the last step.

In the notations specific steps are in some cases prescribed, but these are not to be regarded as obligatory. When no directions are given the choice of step must be determined by the performers themselves. In such cases dancers should remember (1) that the running-step is the normal Country Dance step, and that it is only in comparatively few cases that any other step can be effectively substituted for it ; (2) that slipping and skipping-steps, being compound steps, occupy more time in their execution than the " simple " running-step, and should not therefore be used except in dances of slow or moderate time ; (3) that it is not necessary for every dancer to use the same step at the same time ; nor, again, is it necessary (4) that a single figure should always be danced to one step throughout—the arbitrary change of step in the course of a movement is not only permissible, but is in many cases to be commended.

ARMS AND HANDS.

Nearly all the prescribed arm-movements in the Country Dance relate to the joining of hands. Of ornamental or fanciful movements there are none, nor any of formal design that are devised—like many of the arm-movements of the Morris Dance—to assist the actions of the dancer. Nevertheless, perhaps for this reason, the carriage and manipulation of the hands and arms form a very characteristic feature of the Country Dance.

It may be taken as a general rule that when the arms are not in active use, *i.e.*, when they are not being directly employed for some specific purpose, they should be allowed to swing quietly and loosely by the side. This involves complete relaxation of the muscles that control the shoulder, elbow, and wrist joints, and the capacity to resist sympathetic, involuntary tension in other muscles.

The dancer may sometimes find it necessary to make use of his arms to maintain his balance, *e.g.*, to throw out the outside arm when moving swiftly round a sharp curve. This is permissible, provided that such movements are made only when really necessary, simply, and without exaggeration.

All the prescribed hand and arm movements in the Country Dance have a definite purpose, and in their execution no more is required of the dancer than that he should fulfil this purpose effectively and in the simplest and most direct way. For instance, in " leading " the taking of hands is not a mere formality ; the dancer should actually lead—that is, support his partner, guide and regulate her movement.

THE JOINING OF HANDS.

In linking right hand with right, or left with left, the hands are held sideways (*i.e.*, in a vertical plane), thumbs uppermost, and brought lightly together, not clenched, the four fingers of each hand resting on the palm of the other, and the thumb pressing on the knuckle of the middle finger. The hands should be joined in this manner in leading, in handing in the Hey, and in the Turn with one hand.

In joining inside hands, that is, right hand with left, or left hand with right, *e.g.*, in rings, the Turn, the Poussette, etc., the man holds his hand palm upward, the woman places her hand in his, and the fingers are clasped as before.

When two men or two women join inside hands, it is suggested that the dancer having the lower number should always take the man's position (*i.e.*, give his hand palm upward).

MOVEMENTS OF COURTESY.

THE HONOUR.

This is a formal obeisance made by partners to one another at the conclusion, and sometimes in the course, of the dance. The man bows, head erect, making a slight forward inclination of the body from the hips; the woman, placing her left foot behind the right, makes a quick downward and upward movement by bending and straightening the knees.

The honour should always be made in rhythm with the music and, if possible, in conjunction with some corresponding movement of the feet. The exact way in which this is done depends upon circumstances. The usual method is to place the right foot on the ground twelve inches or so to the side say, on the first beat of the bar, and to bring up the left foot beside it—or, in the case of the woman, behind it—on the following beat when the obeisance is made.

THE SET.

This is a movement of courtesy, addressed by one dancer to another, or more frequently by two dancers to each other simultaneously. It consists of a single to the right sideways, followed by a single to the left back to position (two bars).

THE SET-AND-HONOUR.

This is a lengthened form of the Set occupying four instead of two bars. On the first beat of the first bar the right foot is placed on the ground sideways to the right; on the first beat of the second bar the left foot is brought up beside it and the honour paid in the manner already explained (two bars). These movements are then repeated in the reverse direction, the left foot being moved to the side, the right foot brought up beside it, and the honour paid (two bars, *i.e.*, four bars in all).

THE SIDE.

This is performed by two dancers, usually partners, but not necessarily so. They face each other, and move forward a double obliquely to the right, *i.e.*, passing by the left. On the third step they make a half-turn counter-clockwise, completing the turn on the fourth step as they face one another (two bars). This completes the first half of the movement, and is called *side to the right*. In the second half of the movement, *side to the left*, the dancers retrace their steps along the same tracks, moving obliquely to the left (passing by the right), turn clockwise, and face each other on the fourth step. The whole movement occupies four bars of the music.

The dancers must remember to face each other at the beginning and close of each movement, to pass close to each other, shoulder to shoulder, and always to face in the direction in which they are moving.

ARM WITH THE RIGHT (OR LEFT).

Two performers, usually partners, meet, link right (or left) arms, swing round a complete circle, clockwise (or counter-clockwise) (two bars), separate, and fall back to places (r.s.) (two bars, *i.e.*, four bars in all).

In order that the dancers may give and receive mutual support in the execution of the whole turn, the arms, crooked at right angles, must be linked at the elbows, the dancers leaning slightly away from each other, so as to throw part of their weight on their arms.

THE FIGURES.

FIGURE 1.

HANDS-THREE, HANDS-FOUR, ETC.

Three or more dancers, as directed, form a ring, extend arms, join hands a little above waist-level, and dance round. In the absence of specific instructions to the contrary it is to be understood that one complete circuit is to be danced, clockwise, the performers facing centre.

The dancers should clasp hands firmly, lean outward, and thus support each other. When the movement is followed by a repetition in the reverse direction, counter-clockwise, the dancers may stamp on the first step of the second movement.

Occasionally this figure is performed with backs to the centre, the dancers facing outward.

When space is restricted and the ring reduced in size, and it is no longer feasible to extend the arms, the arms should be raised, sharply bent at the elbows (upper arms horizontal, fore-arms approximately vertical) and the hands joined above head-level. This, too, will be found to be the easier and more convenient method when the movement is slow and formal in character, as is not infrequently the case in back-rings (*e.g.*, the back-ring in " Fye, Nay, Prithee John," p. 122).

FIGURE 2.

THE TURN.

Two dancers face one another, join both hands, swing once round clockwise (unless otherwise directed), separate, and fall back to places.

In turning, performers should clasp hands firmly, arms at full stretch, and lean back so as mutually to give and receive support. If either the skipping-step or running-step be used, the feet should be slightly crossed so that the dancers may face each other squarely throughout the movement.

FIGURE 3.

THE SWING.

This is similar to the preceding movement, the dancers however turning continuously and, on occasion, moving from place to place as directed.

FIGURE 4.

THE TURN WITH RIGHT OR LEFT HAND.

Two dancers join right or left hands, as directed, and move round a complete circle, separate, and fall back to places.

The carriage of the dancers and the position of their arms will depend upon the size of the circle described and the speed with which the figure is executed. When eight steps are allotted to the figure the dancers should describe a large circle, lean slightly towards each other, and join hands above head-level. As the taking of hands in this case is for the purpose of balance rather than support, there is no pull on the arms and no necessity, therefore, to extend them at full stretch. The arms should, accordingly, be held loosely and slightly curved at the elbow (not bent at an angle). If, however, the Turn has to be completed in four steps, the arms should be fully extended and the hands joined a little above waist-level, the dancers leaning away from and supporting each other; while in still faster turns, where the dancers are compelled to turn in a very small circle (as in the Do-Si in the Running Set) they should join hands below waist-level with arms tense and sharply crooked at the elbow.

FIGURE 5.

RIGHT- (OR LEFT-) HANDS-ACROSS.

This is performed usually by four dancers (say, the first and second couples in a longways dance), but occasionally by three or six.

In the first case, first man and second woman join right (or left) hands, while second man and first woman do the same. Holding their hands close together, head-level, the four dancers dance round clockwise (or counter-clockwise), inclining inwards towards the centre, and facing in the direction they are moving.

When three performers only are engaged, two of them join hands and the third places his hand on theirs.

It is to be understood that the dancers make one complete circuit unless specific instructions to the contrary are given.

FIGURE 6.

HALF-POUSSETTE.

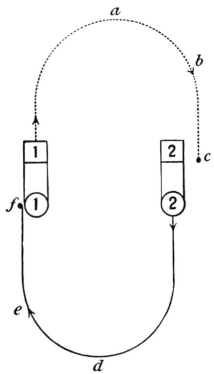

This is performed by two adjacent couples.

Each man faces his partner and takes her by both hands. The arms must be held out straight, and very nearly shoulder high.

First man, pushing his partner before him, moves four steps along dotted line to *a*, and then falls back four steps along the line *a b c* into the second couple's place, pulling his partner after him.

Simultaneously, second man, pulling his partner with him, falls back four steps along unbroken line to *d*, and then moves forward four steps along the line *d e f* into the first couple's place (four bars).

The above movement is called the half-poussette, and is, of course, a progressive figure.

When the half-poussette is followed by a repetition of the same movement, each couple describing a complete circle or ellipse, the figure is called the whole-poussette.

FIGURE 7.

BACK-TO-BACK.

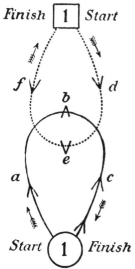

First man and first woman face each other and move forward, the man along the line *a b*, the woman along the dotted line *d e.* They pass by the right, move round each other, back to back, and fall back to places, the man along the line *b c*, the woman along the dotted line *e f*.

The arrow heads in the diagram show the positions of the dancers at the end of each bar, and point in the directions in which they are facing. The arrows alongside the lines show the direction in which the dancers move.

FIGURE 8.

WHOLE-GIP FACING CENTRE.

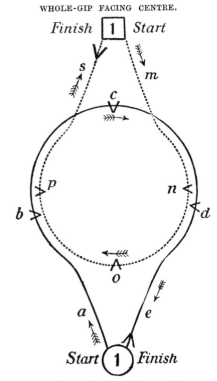

First man moves forward along line *a*, dances round circle *b c d*, facing the centre, and falls back along line *d e* to place;

while first woman dances along dotted line *m*, moves round circle *n o p*, facing the centre, and falls back along dotted line *p s* to place (four bars). In the execution of the running-step the feet will have to be slightly crossed in order that the dancers may face each other squarely throughout the movement.

The arrows and arrow heads have the same signification as in the preceding figure.

FIGURE 9.

WHOLE-GIP FACING OUTWARD.

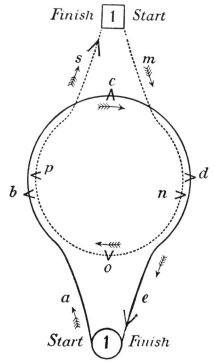

First man moves along line *a* and dances round circle *b c d*, facing outward to place ; while first woman moves along

dotted line *m*, dances round circle *n o p*, facing outward, and
moves along dotted line *p s* to place (four bars).

––––––

THE HEY.

The Hey may be defined as the rhythmical interlacing in
serpentine fashion of two groups of dancers, moving in single
file and in opposite directions.

The figure assumes different forms according to the
disposition of the dancers.   These varieties, however, fall
naturally into two main types according as the track described
by the dancers—disregarding the deviations made by them in
passing one another—is (1) a straight line, or (2) the perimeter
of a closed figure, circle, or ellipse.

The second of these species, as the simpler of the two, will
be first explained.

Figure 10.

THE CIRCULAR HEY.

In the analysis that follows the circle will, for the sake of
convenience, be used throughout to represent the track
described by the dancers in this form of the figure.   In the
round dance the track will of course be a true circle ; while
in the square dance it will become one as soon as the move-

ment has begun. On the other hand, in a longways dance, the formation will be elliptical rather than circular, but this will not affect the validity of the following explanation.

In the circular-hey the dancers, who must be even in number, are stationed at equal distances around the circumference of a circle, facing alternately in opposite directions, thus :—

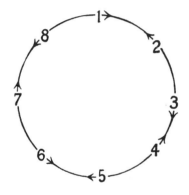

DIAGRAM 4.

Odd numbers face and move round clockwise ; even numbers counter-clockwise. All move at the same rate and, upon meeting, pass alternately by the right and left.

This progression is shown in diagram 5, the dotted and unbroken lines indicating the tracks described respectively by odd and even numbers. It will be seen that in every circuit the two opposing groups of dancers, odd and even, thread through each other twice ; that is, there will be eight

simultaneous passings, or *changes*, as we will call them, in
each complete circuit :—

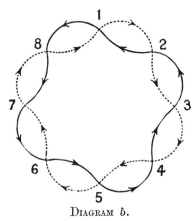

DIAGRAM 5.

This movement is identical with that of the Grand Chain,
except that in the familiar Lancers figure the performers
take hands, alternately right and left, as they pass; whereas,
in the Country Dance hey, "handing," as Playford calls it,
is the exception rather than the rule.

In this form the hey presents no difficulty. No misconcep-
tion can arise so long as (1) the initial dispositions of the
pairs, and (2) the duration of the movement, measured by
circuits or changes, are clearly defined; and instructions on
these two points will always be given in the notation. It
should be understood that in the absence of directions to the
contrary (1) the first pass is by the right, and (2) the dancers
pass without handing.

FIGURE 11.

PROGRESSIVE CIRCULAR HEY.

Sometimes the hey is danced progressively, the dancers
beginning and ending the movement pair by pair, instead of
simultaneously, as above described. This is effected in the
following way :—

The first change is performed by one pair only, say Nos. 1
and 2 (see diagram 4, Fig. 10) ; the second by two pairs,
Nos. 1 and 3, and Nos. 2 and 8 ; the third in like manner by
three pairs, and the fourth by four pairs. At the conclusion
of the fourth change Nos. 1 and 2 will be face to face, each
having traversed half a circuit, and all the dancers will be
actively engaged, thus :—

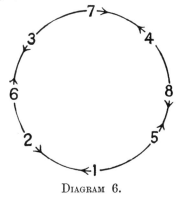

DIAGRAM 6.

The movement now proceeds in the usual way. At the
end of every complete circuit the position will be as follows :—

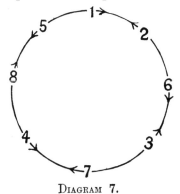

DIAGRAM 7.

The figure is concluded in the following manner :—
Nos. 1 and 2, upon reaching their original places (see
diagram 7), stop and remain neutral for the rest of the
movement.   The others continue dancing until they reach
their proper places, when they, in like manner, stop and
become neutral. This they will do, pair by pair, in the
following order, Nos. 3 and 8, 4 and 7, 5 and 6.   The initial
and final movements thus occupy the same time, *i.e.*, four
changes.

Whenever the progressive hey occurs (1) the initial pair
will be named ; and (2) the duration of the movement,
measured by changes or circuits, will be given in the notation.

FIGURE 12.

THE STRAIGHT HEY.

The dancers stand in a straight line at equi-distant stations,
alternately facing up and down, thus :—

DIAGRAM 8.

Odd numbers face down ; even numbers up.   As in the
circular hey the dancers move at an even rate, and pass each
other alternately by the right and left.   The movement is
shown in diagram 9, the dotted and unbroken lines indicating,
respectively, the upward and downward tracks described by
the dancers :—

DIAGRAM 9.

It will be seen that the dancers after making the last pass
at either end make a whole-turn—bearing to the right if the

last pass was by the right, or to the left if the last pass was by the left—and re-enter the line, now in reverse direction, the first pass after re-entrance being by the same shoulder, right or left, as the preceding one.

When the Straight-hey is performed by three dancers only, we have the form in which the hey occurs most frequently in the Country Dance. On this account it will perhaps be advisable to describe this particular case in detail.

THE STRAIGHT HEY-FOR-THREE.

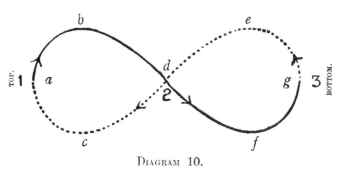

DIAGRAM 10.

No. 1 faces down, Nos. 2 and 3 up.

All simultaneously describe the figure eight, as shown in the above diagram, and return to places, passing along the unbroken line as they move down, and along the dotted line as they move up. At the beginning of the movement, therefore, No. 1 will dance along *a b*, No. 2 along *d c*, and No. 3 along *g e*, *i.e.*, Nos. 1 and 2 will pass by the right, Nos. 1 and 3 by the left.

In order that the dancers may not obstruct one another the two lobes of the figure should be made as broad as time and space will permit.

This is presumably the correct way in which the hey-for-three should be executed in the Country Dance, although we have no direct evidence that it was in fact so danced in Playford's day. Hogarth, however, in his *Analysis of Beauty* (1753), after defining the hey as " a cypher of S's, a number of serpentine lines interlacing and intervolving one another," prints a diagram of the hey-for-three which, although it might have been clearer, seems to show that the way the figure was danced at that period was substantially the same as that described above.

Moreover, Wilson (*The Analysis of Country Dancing*, 1811) also describes the figure and prints a diagram, of which the following— except that for clearness' sake the tracks are differentiated by means of varied lines—is a faithful reproduction :—

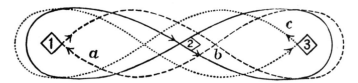

No. 1 moves along the broken line *a* ; No. 2 along the line *b* ; and No. 3 along the dotted line *c*.

Except that the two half-heys are inverted—the two *lower* dancers beginning the movement and passing by the *left*— the method shown in the diagram is precisely the same as that we have above described.

The straight-hey may be performed progressively. It is unnecessary, however, to describe in detail the way in which this is effected, because, in principle, the method is the same as that already explained in Fig. 11.

Playford makes frequent use of the expressions " Single Hey " and " Double Hey." It is difficult to say with certainty what he means by these terms, because he uses them very loosely. Very often they are identical with what we have called the straight- and circular-hey. As, however, this is not always the case, I have, with some reluctance, substituted the terms used above, which are self-explanatory and free from ambiguity.

The figures above described are the commonplaces of the Country Dance, and are to be found, one or other of them, in pretty nearly every dance. The rest—and they are infinite in number and variety—are described in the notations as they occur.

THE TECHNIQUE OF FIGURE-DANCING.

The first requisite of the figure dancer, as has been already pointed out, is the capacity to move hither and thither, freely and easily, with complete control over direction and speed. Having attained this power he must then learn (1) to " time " his movements accurately ; (2) to phrase them in accord with the music ; (3) to blend them into one continuous movement without halts or hesitations ; and (4) to execute them in concert with his fellow-dancers.

Timing.— As the movements and the figures of the dance are but the translation, in terms of bodily action, of the music which accompanies them, the dancer when learning a dance should first of all listen carefully to the tune, and, if possible, memorise it. In particular he should note the number and relative lengths of its several phrases and calculate the number of steps that can be danced to each of them (two in every bar in duple, and three in triple-measure).

In the description of the dances given in the notation it will be found that a definite number of bars, and therefore of steps, is allotted to every figure and to every part of every figure, and it is by this system of measurement by step that the dancers " time " their movements with the music. Every dancer, therefore, must always have in mind not only the form and the shape of the figure he is executing, but the number of steps apportioned to the figure as a whole and to each subsidiary section of which that figure is compounded. So long, however, as he "times" his movements correctly and arrives at his appointed station at the end of each section of the figure, it is for him to determine the precise manner in which he shall distribute his steps in relation to the track or course described. He may, for instance, enlarge his track by taking larger steps, or restrict it by taking shorter ones. In the Gip, for example, the size of the circle described by the two dancers is immaterial so long as, by regulating their speed, they succeed in completing the circuit and regaining their original stations in the prescribed number of steps. When pressed for time the dancer may find it helpful to anticipate a movement, *i.e.*, to start it a beat or so in advance; or *per contra* when he has time in hand, to delay it by taking one or more preliminary "balance-steps" before getting under way. Devices of this kind should, of course, be employed sparingly and never without good reason, as, for example, in the cases above cited, to avoid unseemly scurrying on the one hand or a premature conclusion on the other.

Phrasing.—It is just as necessary for the dancer to phrase his steps and movements as it is for the musician to phrase his notes and strains, or for the writer to punctuate his sentences. The purpose in each case is the same—to define and make intelligible what would otherwise be ambiguous or meaningless. A series of equally accented dance-steps, musical sounds, or verbal syllables, conveys no meaning until by the periodic recurrence of stronger accents the steps, sounds, or words, are separated into groups, co-ordinated, and some sort of relationship established between them.

The writer indicates these groups and their relative values by punctuation; the speaker by pauses, emphasis of particular words, and by the rise and fall of his voice; the musician by slurs or phrases, which define the positions of the rhythmical accents; while the dancer groups his steps in correspondence with the rhythmic phrases of the accompanying music. The dancer, like the musician, must be careful to distinguish between the metrical accents (*i.e.*, the accents or beats within the bar) and the rhythmical accents (of which the bar itself is the unit), the former corresponding to the "foot" in prosody, the latter to the "verse."

Technically, the dancer phrases his movements by gradating the accents which he imparts to his steps, giving the strongest accent to the first step of a group and the weakest to the last. The strength of the step accent depends partly upon foot-spring, but mainly upon body-balance. In a stationary figure like the turn-single, the step-accents are determined solely by the height and energy of the springs with which the steps are made. When, however, the dancer is in motion, the accent of the step depends less upon the strength of the spring forward than upon the momentum generated and controlled by the inclination of the body in the direction of motion. Before beginning a movement from rest, therefore, the dancer should throw his weight on to one foot and adjust the inclination of his body so that the first step of his phrase, which is always the most important, as it is also the strongest, may be made with the requisite emphasis.

The dancer must never make any movement in the dance, however insignificant, that is not phrased, *i.e.*, executed rhythmically in accord with the music. This injunction must be held to apply as much to arm-movements as to steps. For instance, in giving or taking a hand, he should begin the movement in plenty of time—two or three beats beforehand— and raise and move the arm in rhythm with the music.

Continuity. — The directions given in the notation are divided into Parts, figures, etc., only for the sake of clearness of description. The aim of the dancer should be to conceal, not to call attention to these divisions. In learning a dance it will probably be necessary to dissect its movements, to parse, so to speak, each component section ; but in the finished dance these subordinate elements must be pieced together and merged into one continuous movement as complete and organic in structure as the movements of a symphony.

To this end the dancer must think ahead, perceive the relation between that which he is at the moment doing with that which is to follow, so that he may give to the concluding cadence of each subsidiary phrase its just degree of emphasis, and pass on without hesitation to the movement that follows. If he fails in this, his movements will be spasmodic, his phrases isolated and unrelated, and his performance as a whole as unintelligible and difficult to follow as reading aloud by a child who spells out and pronounces with equal emphasis each word as he proceeds.

Concerted movement.—The performer in a concerted dance has not only to consider his own individual movements, but to relate them to those of his companions in the dance. The expert figure-dancer is probably far more conscious of the movements of his fellow-dancers than of his own ; indeed, his pleasure, as well as theirs, depends very largely upon the completeness with which he effaces his own personality and loses himself in the dance.

Although the continuous and accurate adjustment of position by the dancer in a figure-dance is of first-rate importance, it is quite possible to exaggerate it, and by paying too much attention to precision of line and symmetry of figure, to stiffen and formalize the movements, and to give to the dance the appearance of a military drill. The ideal is to steer a middle course. To this end the following general directions will be found useful :—

In line formation each dancer should adjust his position in relation to the dancer on either side. In dual movements, *e.g.*, the Side, Arms, Back-to-back, etc., the distances traversed by each performer should be approximately equal. In the heys—especially the straight-hey-for-three—and the Gip, the performers should describe identically the same track. In the forming of rings the dancers should extend their arms and move round in a circle, edging towards the centre until they are near enough to link hands with the dancers on either side.

STYLE.

The foregoing explanations will, it is hoped, enable the reader to interpret the figures described in the notations that are presently to follow. The dancer should, however, be reminded that technical proficiency has no value except as an aid to artistic expression, and indeed, if it be not so used, the dance will never rise above the level of a physical exercise.

Although in the nature of things it is impossible to instruct the dancer how he may impart æsthetic significance to his physical movements, there are nevertheless certain general considerations to which his attention may profitably be directed. He can, for instance, turn his attention to Style, the cultivation of which will carry him a few steps at any rate along the right road. By style we do not mean polish, *i.e.*, perfected physical movement, but rather the air, the manner with which physical movements are executed. It is partly individual, the expression—that is, voluntary or involuntary—of the dancer's personality, and partly derived from the character of the dance itself.

Although the personal factor is inherent in every human action, and can never, therefore, be entirely eliminated therefrom, it may be, and often is, suppressed to the point where it becomes unconscious, as in walking and other

common activities and habits.   Now the folk-dance, owing
to its corporate, unconscious origin, is essentially an impersonal
dance, a unique instrument for the expression of those ideas
and emotions that are held and felt collectively, but peculiarly
unfitted for the exploitation of personal idiosyncrasies.   The
folk-dance, therefore, is emphatically not the place for the
display of those self-conscious airs and graces, fanciful posings
and so forth, that play so large a part in dances of a more
conventional order.

The dancer must therefore put these aside and seek
elsewhere for material upon which to mould his style, and this
he will find in the character of the dance itself.   He should
note that the Country Dance is less strenuous, less stern, and
less detached than the Morris ; less involved and less intense
than the Sword Dance; but freer, jollier, more intimate, and,
in a sense, more human than either—perhaps because it is
the only one of the three in which both sexes take part.   It is
a mannered dance, gentle and gracious, formal in a simple,
straightforward way, but above all gay and sociable.   The
spirit of merriment, however, although never wholly absent
from the dance, is not always equally obvious.   There are
certain dances that are comparatively quiet and subdued in
style, in which the normal gaiety is toned down to a decorous
suavity ; while between dances of this kind and those of the
more light-hearted variety, there are many that are emotion-
ally intermediate in type.   It should be the aim of the dancer
to feel these temperamental differences, and reflect them in his
manner and style.

The clue to these emotional variations he will, of course,
find in the accompanying music.   The dance is but the interpretation or translation, in terms of bodily action, of the music
upon which it is woven, just as the melody of the song is
primarily the expression of the text.   Music moreover is the
predominant partner of the union ; there can be no dance

without music. This intimate relationship between the music and the dance and, in a sense, the subservience of the latter to the former, must always be present to the mind of the dancer. Not only must his rhythms accord with those of the music, as has already been pointed out, but his style, the character that he gives to his movements, must also be in harmony with the character of the music.

The application of this principle, viz., the subordination of the dance to the music, is imperative, especially in the case of the dances in the present volume. For the Playford dances, despite the number and variety of their figures, are very persistent in type, and were it not for the wide range of the emotional content of the tunes it would be difficult to give to them the necessary variety of treatment.

It should be added that any spectacular qualities that the Country Dance may possess are fortuitous, or, rather, the inevitable outcome of the perfect fashioning of means to end. Its beauty, being implicit, needs, therefore, no artificial embellishment. An elaborate theatrical setting would be as irrelevant and impertinent as for the dancers to deck themselves in rich and fanciful costumes. All that the dancers need is plenty of space, an even, non-slippery floor, and dresses which will allow to the body and limbs complete freedom of action.

NOTATION.

ROSE IS WHITE AND ROSE IS RED.

Round for as many as will; in six parts (1st Ed., **1650**).

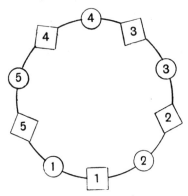

MUSIC.		MOVEMENTS.
		FIRST PART.
A1	1—4	All take hands, move forward a double to centre and fall back a double to places.
	5—8	Partners set and turn single.
A2	1—8	All that again.
		SECOND PART. (Progressive.)
A1	1—4	First couple leads forward a double to second man and falls back a double.
	5—8	First couple and second man hands-three.
A2	1—4	First couple leads forward a double to second woman and falls back a double.
	5—8	First couple and second woman hands-three.

ROSE IS WHITE AND ROSE IS RED—*continued.*

MUSIC.		MOVEMENTS.
		THIRD PART.
A1	1—4	Partners side.
	5—8	Partners set and turn single.
A2	1—8	All that again.
		FOURTH PART. (Progressive.)
A1	1—4	As in A1, Second Part.
	5—8	First couple and second man the straight-hey (first man in the middle passing second man by the left).
A2	1—4	As in A2, Second Part.
	5—8	First couple and second woman the straight-hey (first man passing second woman by the left).
		FIFTH PART.
A1	1—4	Partners arm with the right.
	5—8	Partners set and turn single.
A2	1—4	Partners arm with the left.
	5—8	Partners set and turn single.
		SIXTH PART. (Progressive.)
A1	1—2	First man and first woman, joining inside hands, make an arch and move forward a double to second man; while second man moves forward a double and passes under the arch.
	3—4	All three make a half-turn and repeat the movement in the reverse direction.
	5—8	The two men turn their partners.
A2	1—8	As in A1 with second woman instead of second man.

PEPPERS BLACK.

Round for as many as will; in four parts (1st Ed., 1650).

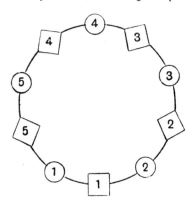

	MUSIC.	MOVEMENTS.
		First Part.
A	1—8	Hands all eight slips clockwise and eight slips counter-clockwise to places.
B	1—4	Partners set and turn single.
	5—8	That again.
		Second Part. (Progressive.)
A	1—4	First couple leads forward a double to second couple and falls back a double.
	5—8	That again.
B	1—4	First man turns second woman; while second man turns first woman.
	5—8	First and second men turn their partners.

PEPPERS BLACK—*continued.*

MUSIC.		MOVEMENTS.
		THIRD PART. (Progressive.)
A	1—8	As in Second Part.
B	1—8	First and second couples circular hey (four changes), partners facing.
		FOURTH PART. (Progressive.)
A	1 – 2	First man and first woman, joining inside hands, move forward a double to second couple.
	3—4	The second man linking his right hand with first man's left, all three fall back a double.
	5—8	The three, still holding hands, move forward a double and fall back a double.
B	1—4	First man, raising his left arm and making an arch with second man, makes a whole turn counter-clockwise on his axis and swings his partner round under the arch back to her place.
	5—8	First man, raising his right arm and making an arch with his partner, makes a whole turn clockwise on his axis and swings second man under the arch back to his place.
		N.B.—*It is suggested that the movements in this Part be repeated, the second woman (instead of the second man) linking right hand with first man's left and doing as second man did.*

MILL-FIELD

Round for as many as will; in two parts (1st Ed., 1650).

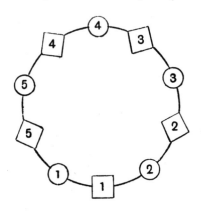

MUSIC.		MOVEMENTS.
		FIRST PART.
A	1—8	Hands-all eight slips clockwise and eight slips counter-clockwise to places.
B	1—4	Partners set and turn single.
	5—8	That again.
		SECOND PART.
		(Progressive.)
A1	1—2	First man and first woman make an arch and lead a double forward to second man; while second man moves forward a double and passes under the arch.
	3—4	First man turns his partner half-way round.
	5—6	As in bars 1—2 in reverse direction to places.

MILL-FIELD — *continued.*

MUSIC.		MOVEMENTS.
		SECOND PART—*continued.*
A1	7—8	First man turns his partner half-way round.
B1	1—4	First couple and second man set and turn single.
	5—8	That again.
A2	1—2	As in A1, first and second men making the arch and leading to first woman.
	3—4	First and second men arm with the right half-way round.
	5—6	As in bars 1—2 in reverse direction to places.
	7—8	First and second men arm with the left half-way round.
B2	1—8	As in B1.
A3	1—2	As in A1, second man and first woman making the arch and leading to first man.
	3—4	Second man turns first woman half-way round.
	5—6	As in bars 1—2 in reverse direction to places.
	7—8	Second man turns first woman half-way round.
B3	1—8	As in B1.
A4, B4, A5, B5, A6, and B6		As in A1—B3, second woman doing as second man did.

SAGE LEAF.
Round for as many as will (4th Ed., **1670**).

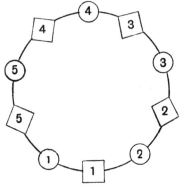

MUSIC.		MOVEMENTS.
A1	1—4	Hands-all eight slips clockwise.
A1	(repeat)	Hands-all eight slips counter-clockwise to places.
B	1—4	The men move forward a double to centre and fall back a double to places.
	5—8	The women do likewise.
C	1—4	First couple leads forward a double to centre and falls back a double.
	5—8	First man and first woman turn with right hands.
(Played as many times as there are couples)		*This figure is then performed in turn by each of the other couples.*
D	1—4	Each man turns his partner with the right hand, passes on and turns the next woman on his right in a like manner and proceeds in this way round the ring, counter-clockwise to his place.
(Played as many times as there are couples)		

SAGE LEAF—*continued.*

MUSIC.	MOVEMENTS.
B, C, & D (repeated)	*The three figures B, C, and D are executed as many times as there are couples. In the first repetition, however, the second couple, instead of the first, will initiate the C movement, in the second repetition the third couple, and so on. After the last repetition of these three figures the dance is brought to a conclusion as follows :—*
A2 1—8	Hands-all eight slips clockwise.
A2 (repeat)	Hands-all eight slips counter-clockwise to places.

MUNDESSE.

Round for six ; in seven parts (1st Ed., 1650).

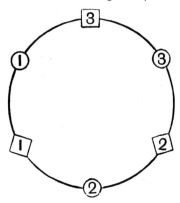

MUSIC.		MOVEMENTS.
		First Part.
A1	1—4	Hands-six eight slips clockwise.
	5—8	Partners set and turn single.
A2	1—4	Hands-six eight slips counter-clockwise.
	5—8	Partners set and turn single.
B	1—4	First man sets to his partner and turns single.
	5—8	First woman sets to her partner and turns single.
C	1—2	First man honours his partner.
	3—4	Second man the same.
	5—6	Third man the same.
	7—8	Partners honour each other.
D	1—4	Partners turn.
	5—8	Each man turns the woman on his left.

MUNDESSE—*continued.*

MUSIC.		MOVEMENTS.
		SECOND PART.
A1	1—8	First man leads his partner forward eight steps and falls back eight steps.
A2	1—8	First man leads his partner forward between second and third couples ; they cast off, the man to his left, the woman to her right, and return to places, passing behind the third and second couples respectively.
B	1—4	First woman sets to second man and turns single.
	5—8	Second man sets to first woman and turns single.
C	1—2	First woman honours the man on her right.
	3—4	Second woman the same.
	5—6	Third woman the same.
	7—8	Partners honour.
D	1—8	As in First Part.
		THIRD PART.
A1 and **A2**		As in Second Part, first woman leading second man between third man and third woman.
B	1—4	Second man sets to his partner and turns single.
	5—8	Second woman sets to her partner and turns single.
C	1—2	Second man honours his partner.
	3—4	Third man the same.
	5—6	First man the same.
	7—8	Partners honour.
D	1—8	As in First Part.

MUNDESSE—*continued.*

MUSIC.		MOVEMENTS.
		FOURTH PART.
A1 and **A2**		As in Second Part, second man leading his partner between first and third couples.
B	1—4	Second woman sets to third man and turns single.
	5—8	Third man sets to second woman and turns single.
C	1—2	Second woman honours the man on her right.
	3—4	Third woman the same.
	5—6	First woman the same.
	7—8	Partners honour.
D	1—8	As in First Part.
		FIFTH PART.
A1 and **A2**		As in Second Part, second woman leading third man between first man and first woman.
B	1—4	Third man sets to his partner and turns single.
	5—8	Third woman sets to her partner and turns single.
C	1—2	Third man honours his partner.
	3—4	First man the same.
	5—6	Second man the same.
	7—8	Partners honour.
D	1—8	As in First Part.

MUNDESSE—*continued.*

MUSIC.		MOVEMENTS.
		SIXTH PART.
A1 and **A2**		As in Second Part, third man leading his partner between first and second couples.
B	1—4	Third woman sets to first man and turns single.
	5—8	First man sets to third woman and turns single.
C	1—2	Third woman honours the man on her right.
	8—4	First woman the same.
	5—6	Second woman the same.
	7—8	Partners honour.
D	1—8	As in First Part.
		SEVENTH PART.
A1 and **A2**		As in Second Part, third woman leading first man between second man and second woman.
B	1—8	As in First Part.
C	1—8	As in First Part.
D	1—8	As in First Part.

EPPING FOREST.

Round for six; in three parts (4th Ed., 1670).

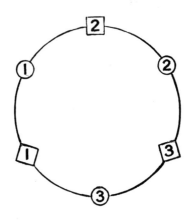

MUSIC.		MOVEMENTS.
		FIRST PART.
A1	1—4	Hands-six eight slips clockwise.
	5—8	Partners set and turn single.
A2	1—4	Hands-six eight slips counter-clockwise to places.
	5—8	Partners set and turn single.
B	1—4	Men set-and-honour to partners.
	5—8	Men set-and-honour each to the woman on his left.
C	1—4	Men turn their partners.
	5—8	Men turn each the woman on his left.

EPPING FOREST—*continued.*

MUSIC.		MOVEMENTS.
		SECOND PART.
A1	1—4	Partners side.
	5—8	Partners set and turn single.
A2	1—8	All that again.
B and **C**		As in First Part.
		THIRD PART.
A1	1—4	Partners arm with the right.
	5—8	Partners set and turn single.
A2	1—4	Partners arm with the left.
	5—8	Partners set and turn single.
B and **C**		As in First Part.

THE MAID IN THE MOON.
Round for six; in three parts (4th Ed., 1670).

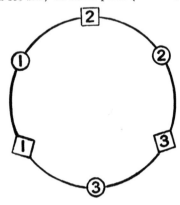

MUSIC.		MOVEMENTS.
		FIRST PART.
A1	1—4	All take hands, move forward a double to centre and fall back a double to places.
	5—8	Partners set and turn single.*
A2	1—8	All that again.
B1	1—2	First man and third woman meet and join right hands.
	3—4	Second man and first woman do the same.
	5—6	Third man and second woman do the same.
	7—10	Right-hands-across once round to places.
B2	1—2	First man and third woman honour.
	3—4	Second man and first woman do the same.
	5—6	Third man and second woman do the same.
	7—10	Right-hands-across to places.

* The interpolation of "Set and turn single" in A1 and A2 of each Part is rendered necessary by the change of tune.

THE MAID IN THE MOON—*continued.*

MUSIC.		MOVEMENTS.
		SECOND PART.
A1	1— 4	Partners side.
	5—8	Partners set and turn single.
A2	1—8	All that again.
B1	1—10	As in First Part.
B2	1—2	First man and second woman honour.
	3—4	Second man and third woman honour.
	5—6	Third man and first woman honour.
	7—10	Right-hands-across to places.
		THIRD PART.
A1	1—4	Partners arm with the right.
	5—8	Partners set and turn single.
A2	1—4	Partners arm with the left.
	5—8	Partners set and turn single.
B1	1—10	As in B1, First Part, but joining left hands and going left-hands-across.
B2	1—2	First man and first woman honour.
	3—4	Second man and second woman honour.
	5—6	Third man and third woman honour.
	7—10	Left-hands-across.

DISSEMBLING LOVE, OR THE LOST HEART.

Longways for six; in three parts (1st Ed., 1650).

1	2	3
①	②	③

MUSIC.		MOVEMENTS.
		FIRST PART.
A	1—4	Partners lead up a double and fall back a double to places.
	5—8	That again.
B1	1—4	First man and woman cross over, cast down, cross over between the second and third couples, cast down and fall into the third places, second and third couples moving up into the first and second places, respectively (sk.s.).
B2	1—4	Second couple does as first couple did in B1.
B3	1—4	Third couple the same.
		SECOND PART.
A	1—4	Partners side.
	5—8	That again.
B1	1—2	Straight-hey on the men's side and on the women's side, two changes (*i.e.*, the top dancer moving down two places to the bottom, the other two each moving up one place).

DISSEMBLING LOVE—*continued.*

MUSIC.		MOVEMENTS.
		SECOND PART—*continued.*
B1	3—4	All turn single.
B2	1—4	As in B1.
B3	1—4	As in B1 to places.
		THIRD PART.
A	1—4	Partners arm with the right.
	5—8	Partners arm with the left.
B1	1—2	The middle man falling back, the men go hands-three a third of the way round (*i.e.*, the top man going down two places to the bottom, the other two each moving up one place); while the women go hands-three counter-clockwise a third of the way round.
	3—4	All turn single.
B1	1—4	As in B1.
B2	1—4	As in B1 to places.

THE NIGHT PIECE.

Longways for six; in three parts (1st Ed., 1650).

1	2	3
①	②	③

MUSIC.		MOVEMENTS.
		FIRST PART.
A	1—4	Partners lead up a double and fall back a double to places.
	5—8	That again.
B1	1—4	Top and bottom couples face, move forward and pass each other (opposites passing by the right) and fall, the top couple into the bottom place, the bottom couple into the middle place; while the middle man and woman fall back and slip up into the first place.
B2	1—4	As in **B1**.
B3	1—4	As in B1 to places.
		SECOND PART.
A	1—4	Partners side.
	5—8	That again.
B1	1—4	Top man and top woman cross over, cast down, cross again between middle and bottom couples and cast down into the bottom place (sk. s.), the other couples each moving up one place.

THE NIGHT PIECE—*continued.*

MUSIC.		MOVEMENTS.
		SECOND PART—*continued.*
B2	1—4	As in B1.
B3	1—4	As in B1 to places.
		THIRD PART.
A	1—4	Partners arm with the right.
	5 8	Partners arm with the left.
B1	1—2	First man changes places with second woman.
	3 – 4	First woman changes places with second man; while third man changes places with his partner.
B2	1—2	First man changes places with third woman.
	3—4	First woman changes places with third man; while second man changes places with his partner.
B3	1—4	Partners set and turn single.
		The following variation of the last three movements is suggested in order that the dancers may finish in their proper places.
B1	1—4	In the first two bars first man changes places with second woman, in the next two bars first woman changes places with second man; while third man and third woman cross over and cast up into the first place (improper).
B2	1—4	Third woman changes places with second man (2 bars) and third man with second woman (2 bars); while first man and first woman cross over and cast up to places.
B3	1 – 4	Partners set and turn single.

JACK A LENT.

Longways for six ; in six parts (1st Ed., **1650**).

1	2	3
①	②	③

MUSIC.		MOVEMENTS.
		FIRST PART.
A1	1—4	Partners lead up a double and fall back a double to places.
	5—8	That again.
B1	1—4	Top dancer on the men's side changes places with the middle dancer on the opposite side and both turn single.
	5—8	The same dancer changes places with the bottom dancer on the opposite side and both turn single.
A2	1—8	As in A1.
B2	1—8	Top dancer on the women's side does as the top dancer on the men's side did in B1.
A3	1—8	As in A1.
B3	1—8	As in B1.
A4	1—8	As in A1.
B4	1—8	As in B2.
A5	1—8	As in A1.
B5	1—8	As in B1.
A6	1—8	As in A1.
B6	1—8	As in B2 to places.

JACK A LENT—*continued.*

MUSIC.		MOVEMENTS.
		SECOND PART.
A1	1—8	As in A1, First Part.
B1	1—8	First man and woman cross over, cast down and cross over again between second and third couples, cast down below the third couple and fall into the third place (sk.s.), the second and third couples moving up one place.
A2	1—8	As in A1.
B2	1—8	Second couple does as first couple did in B1.
A3	1—8	As in A1.
B3	1—8	Third couple does as first couple did in B1.
		THIRD PART.
A1	1—8	As in A1, First Part.
B1	Bar 1	Partners face and join both hands. First and second couples change places, the first couple going between and under the arms of the second couple (sk.s.).
	Bar 2	First and third couples change places, third couple going under the arms of the first couple.
	Bar 3	Second and third couples change places, second couple going under the arms of the third couple.
	Bar 4	First and second couples change places, first couple going under the arms of the second couple.
	Bar 5	First and third couples change places, third couple going under the arms of the first couple.

JACK A LENT—*continued.*

MUSIC.		MOVEMENTS.
		THIRD PART—*continued.*
	Bar 6	Second and third couples change places, second couple going under the arms of the third couple.
	7—8	First man and first woman cast down to the bottom (sk.s.), second and third couples moving up one place.
A2	1—8	As in A1.
B2	1—8	As in B1, second and third couples beginning the movement, and second man and woman casting down.
A3	1—8	As in A1.
B3	1—8	As in B1 to places, third and first couples beginning the movement, and third man and woman casting down.
		FOURTH PART.
A1	1—8	As in A1, First Part.
B1	1—8	First man goes down the middle (r.s.), turns third man half-way round clockwise, and the second man the whole way round counter-clockwise, and then casts down to the bottom (sk.s.), second and third men moving up one place ; while first woman goes down the middle, turns third woman half-way round counter-clockwise, and the second woman the whole way round clockwise, and then casts down to the bottom (sk.s.), second and third women moving up one place.
A2	1—8	As in A1, First Part.

JACK A LENT—*continued.*

MUSIC.		MOVEMENTS.
		FOURTH PART – *continued.*
B2	1—8	As in B1, second man and second woman going down the middle, turning the two men and women, respectively, and casting off.
A3	1—8	As in A1, First Part.
B3	1—8	As in B1 to places, third man and third woman going down the middle, turning, and casting off.
		FIFTH PART.
A1	1—4	First man and last woman meet, turn, and fall back to places.
	5 – 8	First woman and last man do the same.
B1	1—8	First man goes back two steps, moves down the middle, turns the last man once-and-a-half round and falls into the last place on the men's side, second and third men moving up one place; while first woman goes down the middle, turns the last woman once-and-a-half round and falls into the last place on her own side, second and third women moving up one place.
A2	1—8	As in A1, second man turning first woman, and second woman turning first man.
B2	1—8	As in B1, second man and second woman going down the middle, turning first man and first woman, respectively, and falling into the bottom places.
A3	1—8	As in A1, third man turning second woman, and third woman turning second man.

JACK A LENT—*continued.*

MUSIC.		MOVEMENTS.
		FIFTH PART—*continued.*
B3	1—8	As in B1, third man and third woman going down, turning second man and second woman respectively, and falling into their own places.
		SIXTH PART.
A1	1—4	Partners lead up a double and fall back a double to places.
	5—8	That again.
B1	1—4	Partners set and turn single.
	5—8	That again.

THE WHISH.

Longways for six; in three parts (1st Ed., 1650).

| 1 | 2 | 3 |

| ① | ② | ③ |

MUSIC.		MOVEMENTS.
		FIRST PART.
A1	1—4	Partners lead up a double and fall back a double to places.
	5—6	Partners face and set to each other, falling back as they do so.
	Bar 7	Partners move forward and meet.
A2	1—7	All that again.
A3	1—4	The second man leads first man between the first and second women and casts off to his place, the first man doing likewise.
	5—7	First and second men arm with the left.
A4	1—7	As in A3, the second man leading third man between the second and third women, and arming him with the left.
A5	1—4	As in A3, the second woman leading first woman between the first and second men.
	5—7	First and second women arm with the right.
A6	1—7	As in A5, the second woman leading third woman between the second and third men, and arming her with the right.

THE WHISH—*continued.*

MUSIC.		MOVEMENTS.
		SECOND PART.
A1	1—4	Partners side.
	5—7	As in A1, First Part.
A2	1—7	All that again.
A3	1—4	Second man leads his partner between first man and first woman and casts off to his place, his partner doing likewise.
	5—7	Second man turns his partner.
A4	1—7	As in A3, second man leading his partner between third man and third woman, and turning her.
A5 and **A6**		As in A3 and A4, First Part.
A7 and **A8**		As in A5 and A6, First Part.
		THIRD PART.
A1	1—4	Partners arm with the right.
	5—7	As in A1, First Part.
A2	1—4	Partners arm with the left.
	5—7	As in A1, First Part.
A3	1—7	The second couple goes the Figure-8 through the first couple (sk.s.), second man crossing over and passing clockwise round first woman and counter-clockwise round first man, second woman crossing over and passing counter-clockwise round first man and clockwise round first woman.

THE WHISH—*continued.*

MUSIC.	MOVEMENTS.
	THIRD PART—*continued.*
A4 1—7	The second couple goes the Figure-8 through the third couple (sk.s.), the second man crossing over and passing counter-clockwise round third woman and clockwise round third man, the second woman crossing over and passing clockwise round third man and counter-clockwise round third woman.
A5, **A6**, **A7,** and **A8**	As in A3, A4, A5, and A6, First Part.

MALL PEATLY.

Longways for eight; in three parts (4th Ed., 1670).

| 1 | 2 | 3 | 4 |
| (1) | (2) | (3) | (4) |

MUSIC.		MOVEMENTS.
		FIRST PART.
A	1—4	Partners lead up a double and fall back a double to places.
	5—8	That again.
B1	1—2	First man sets to first woman; while fourth man sets to fourth woman.
	3—4	First man sets to second woman; while fourth man sets to third woman.
	5—10	First man heys with the third and fourth women, five changes, passing fourth woman by the right, and falls into the last place on the men's side; while fourth man heys with the first and second women, five changes, passing first woman by the left, and falls into the top place on his own side (sk.s.).
B2	1—10	As in B1 to places, fourth man doing as the first man did, and first man as the fourth.

MALL PEATLY—*continued.*

MUSIC.		MOVEMENTS.
		SECOND PART.
A	1—4	Partners side.
	5—8	That again.
B1	1—2	First woman sets to first man ; while fourth woman sets to fourth man.
	3—4	First woman sets to second man ; while fourth woman sets to third man.
	5—10	First woman heys with third and fourth men, five changes, passing fourth man by the left, and falls into the last place on her own side ; while fourth woman heys with first and second men, five changes, passing first man by the right, and falls into the first place on her own side (sk.s.).
B2	1—10	As in B1, to places, fourth woman doing as the first woman did, and first woman as the fourth.
		THIRD PART.
A	1—4	Partners arm with the right.
	5—8	Partners arm with the left.
D1	1—2	First man and fourth woman set to their partners.
	3—4	First man sets to second woman ; while fourth woman sets to third man.

MALL PEATLY—*continued.*

MUSIC.	MOVEMENTS.
	THIRD PART—*continued.*
5—10	First man heys with second and third women, five changes, passing third woman by the right, and falls into the last place on his own side; while fourth woman heys with second and third men, seven changes, passing second man by the right, and falls into the first place on her own side—second, third, and fourth men moving up one place; first, second, and third women moving down one place.
B2 1—2	First man sets to third woman; while fourth woman sets to second man.
3—4	First man sets to second woman; while fourth woman sets to third man.
5—10	First man heys with first and second women, five changes, passing first woman by the left, and falls into his proper place; while fourth woman heys with third and fourth men, five changes, passing fourth man by the left, and falls into her own place—second, third, and fourth men moving down one place; first, second, and third women moving up one place.

THE SHEPHERD'S DAUGHTER.

Longways for eight; in three parts (2nd Ed., 1652).

$$\boxed{1} \qquad \boxed{2} \qquad \boxed{3} \qquad \boxed{4}$$

$$\textcircled{1} \qquad \textcircled{2} \qquad \textcircled{3} \qquad \textcircled{4}$$

MUSIC.		MOVEMENTS.
		FIRST PART.
A	1— 4	Partners lead up a double and fall back a double to places.
	5— 8	That again.
B	1—4	First and second men, joining inside hands, lead a double to left wall, change hands, and lead back again, the first and second women doing the same; while third and fourth women lead a double to right wall, change hands and lead back again, third and fourth men doing the same.
	5—8	First and second couples lead up a double, change hands and lead back to places; while third and fourth couples lead down a double, change hands and lead back to places.
C	1—4	First and third men turn second and fourth women respectively; while second and fourth men turn first and third women (sk.s.).
	5—8	Partners turn (sk.s.).

THE SHEPHERD'S DAUGHTER—*continued.*

MUSIC.		MOVEMENTS.
		SECOND PART.
A	1—4	Partners side.
	5—8	That again.
B and **C**		As in First Part.
		THIRD PART.
A	1—4	Partners arm with the right.
	5—8	Partners arm with the left.
B and **C**		As in First Part.

THE SLIP.

Longways for eight; in two parts (1st Ed., 1650).

MUSIC.		MOVEMENTS.
		FIRST PART.
A	1—4	All, facing up, set-and-honour to the Presence.
	5—8	Partners set-and-honour.
B1	1 - 2	First and second men, joining inside hands, fall back a double, their partners doing the same; while third and fourth men and their partners do the same.
	3—4	Releasing hands, partners set, falling back with the single on the right foot, and moving forward with the single on the left.
	5 - 8	Partners cross over and change places.
B2	1—8	Same again to places.
		SECOND PART.
A	1—4	Top man leads his partner a double half-way down the middle and honours her.
	5—8	Top man leads his partner a double to the bottom and honours her (the other three couples moving up one place).
B1 and **2**		As in First Part.
		These movements are repeated three times to places.

THE MULBERRY GARDEN.

Longways for as many as will; in two parts (4th Ed., **1670**).

| 1 | 2 | 3 | 4 | • • • • |
| ① | ② | ③ | ④ | • • • • |

MUSIC.		MOVEMENTS.
		FIRST PART.
A	1—4	Partners lead up a double and fall back a double to places.
	5—8	That again.
B	1—4	Partners face. All fall back a double and move forward a double to places.
	5—8	Partners turn.
		SECOND PART. (Duple minor-set.)
A	1—4	First and second men go back-to-back with their partners.
	5—8	First and second men go back-to-back; while first and second women do the same.
B	1—2	Hands-four half-way round (sl.s.).
	3—4	Partners change places (progressive).
	5—8	Second couple casts down into second place and leads up the middle to first place; while first couple leads up the middle to first place and casts down into second place.

SATURDAY NIGHT AND SUNDAY MORN.

Longways for as many as will; in three parts (1st Ed., 1650).

MUSIC.		MOVEMENTS.
		First Part.
A	1—4	Partners lead up a double and fall back a double to places.
	5—8	That again.
B	1—4	Partners set and turn single.
	5—8	That again.
		Second Part. (Duple minor-set.)
A	1—4	First man and first woman whole-gip facing centre, clockwise (Fig. 8, p. 36); while second man and second woman do the same.
	5—8	First and second men whole-gip facing centre, counter-clockwise; while first and second women do the same.
B	1—2	First man changes places with second woman.
	3—4	First woman changes places with second man.
	5—6	Partners change places (progressive).
	7—8	Partners set.

SATURDAY NIGHT—*continued.*

MUSIC.		MOVEMENTS.
		THIRD PART. (Duple minor-set.)
A	1—2	First man and first woman, joining right hands, move down a double ; while second man and second woman, joining right hands and making an arch, move up a double, the first couple passing under their arms.
	3—4	Both couples return to places, second couple passing under the arch made by first couple.
	5　8	First man, joining inside hands with second man, casts off, followed by second man, and returns up the middle to his place ; while the two women, joining inside hands, do the same (sk.s.).
B	1—2	Partners change places.
	3—4	The two men change places ; while the two women do the same.
	5—6	Partners change places (progressive).
	7—8	Partners set.
		Playford gives a Fourth Part which is omitted in the text.

THE MAID PEEPED OUT AT THE WINDOW,
OR
THE FRIAR IN THE WELL.

Longways for as many as will; in three parts (1st Ed., 1650).

MUSIC.		MOVEMENTS.
		FIRST PART.
A	1—4	Partners lead up a double and fall back a double to places.
	5—8	That again.
B1	1—4	First man, followed by the rest of the men, casts off to the bottom of the Set; while first woman followed by the rest of the women, does the same (sk.s.).
	5—8	Partners set and turn single.
B2	1—4	As in B1, casting up to places.
	5—8	Partners set and turn single.
		SECOND PART.
A	1—4	Partners side.
	5—8	That again.
B1	1—2	All face up. The men go four slips to their right on to the women's side, while the women go four slips to their left, on to the men's side, the men passing in front of their partners.
	3—4	All move up a double.
	5—8	Partners set and turn single.

THE MAID PEEPED OUT—*continued.*

MUSIC.		MOVEMENTS.
		SECOND PART—*continued.*
B2	1—2	All face down. The men go four slips to their right on to their own side, while the women go four slips to their left on to their own side, the women passing in front of their partners.
	3—4	All move down a double.
	5—8	Partners set and turn single.
		THIRD PART.
A	1—4	Partners arm with the right.
	5—8	Partners arm with the left.
B1	1—4	All couples half-poussette, odd couples changing places with even couples, the former going first toward the right wall, the latter toward the left wall.
	5—8	All set and turn single.
B2	1—4	As in B1 to places, odd couples going first toward left wall, even couples toward right wall.
	5—8	Partners set and turn single.

DRIVE THE COLD WINTER AWAY.

Longways for as many as will; in three parts (1st Ed., 1650).

1		2		3		4		•	•	•	•
①		②		③		④		•	•	•	•

MUSIC.		MOVEMENTS.
		FIRST PART.
A	1—4	Partners lead up a double and fall back a double to places.
	5—8	That again.
B1	1—8	First man takes two steps backward and moves down the middle (r.s.), turns the last woman but one counter-clockwise and then the last woman clockwise (sk.s.), falling back into the last place on his own side (r.s.); while the second man, followed by the rest of the men, crosses over, passes between the first and second women, casts off to his left and goes down the men's side, meeting the first man (sk.s.).
B2	1—8	First man takes two steps backward and then moves up the middle (r.s.), turns the second woman clockwise and then the first woman counter-clockwise (sk.s.), falling back into his own place (r.s.); while the second man, followed by the rest of the men, crosses over, passes between the last two women, casts off to his right and moves up the men's side to his place (sk.s.).

DRIVE THE COLD WINTER AWAY—*continued.*

MUSIC.		MOVEMENTS.

SECOND PART.

A 1—4 Partners side.

   5—8 That again.

B1 1—8 First woman takes two steps backward and moves down the middle (r.s.), turns the last man but one clockwise and the last man counter-clockwise (sk.s.), falling back into the last place on her own side (r.s.); while the second woman, followed by the rest of the women, crosses over, passes between the first and second men, casts off to her right and dances down her own side, meeting first woman (sk.s.).

B2 1—8 First woman takes two steps backward, moves up the middle (r.s.), turns the second man counter-clockwise, the first man clockwise (sk.s.) and falls back into her own place (r.s.); while the second woman, followed by the rest of the women, crosses over, passes between the last two men, casts off to her left and dances up the women's side to her place (sk.s.).

THIRD PART.

A 1—4 Partners arm with the right.

   5—8 Partners arm with the left.

B1 and **B2** As in First Part.

MAD ROBIN.

Longways for as many as will; in one part (7th Ed., 1686)

| 1 | 2 | 3 | 4 | • • • • |
| ① | ② | ③ | ④ | • • • • |

MUSIC.		MOVEMENTS.
		(Duple minor-set.)
A1	1—8	First man turns second woman with the right hand, his partner with the left hand and then casts down into second place, second man moving up into first place.
A2	1—8	First woman turns her partner with the left hand, the second man with the right hand and then casts down into second place, second woman moving up into first place (progressive).
B1	1—4	First woman moves up the middle and casts down to the second place; while the first man casts up and moves down the middle into the second place.
	5—8	First man turns his partner.
B2	1—4	First man moves up the middle and casts down to the same place ; while his partner casts up and moves down the middle to her place.
	5—8	First man turns his partner.

NEVER LOVE THEE MORE.

Longways for as many as will;   in two parts (7th Ed., 1686).

1	2	3	4	• • • •
①	②	③	④	• • • •

MUSIC.	MOVEMENTS.
	FIRST PART.
A 1—4	All face up and set-and-honour to the Presence.
5—8	Partners set-and honour.
9—12	Partners lead up a double and **fall** back a double to places.
13—16	That again.
	SECOND PART. (Duple minor-set.)
A1 1—4	Partners go back-to-back passing by the right.
5—8	That again passing by the left.
9—16	First man and woman go the Figure-8 through second couple, first man passing counter-clockwise round second woman and clockwise round second man to place; while first woman passes clockwise round second man and counter-clockwise round second woman to place (sk.s.).
A2 1—2	Hands four half-way round (sl.s.).
3—4	All fall back a double.
5—8	Partners cross over and change places (progressive).
9—12	Right-hands-across.
13—16	Left-hands-across.

SLAUGHTER HOUSE.

Longways for as many as will; in one part (8th Ed., 1703)

MUSIC.		MOVEMENTS.
		(Duple minor-set.)
A1	1—4	First couple and second woman hands-three.
	5—8	Second couple and first man hands-three.
A2	1—4	First man and first woman cross over, cast down into second place (improper), move up and stand between second couple, four abreast.
	5—8	All take hands, move forward a double and fall back a double, the first couple falling into second place (improper), the second couple into first place (proper).
B	1—4	First man crosses over, passes counter-clockwise round second man and moves into second place on his own side; while first woman crosses over, passes clockwise round second woman and moves into second place on her own side.
	5—8	First and second couples circular-hey, three changes, to places, partners facing.
C	1—4	First couple leads down between second couple and casts up to places.
	5—6	On the first beat of each bar all four clap their own hands, partners clapping right hands on the second beat of the fifth bar, and left hands on the second beat of the sixth bar.
	7—8	First couple casts down into second place, second couple moving up into first place (progressive).

THE SIEGE OF LIMERICK.

Longways for as many as will; in one part (10th Ed., 1698).

MUSIC.		MOVEMENTS.
		N.B.—*The tune is in triple time, i.e., three steps to the bar.*
		(Duple minor-set.)
A	1—4	First man casts down below second man crosses over and passes clockwise round second woman into the second place on his own side, the second man moving up into first place.
	5—8	First woman casts down below second woman, crosses over and passes counter clockwise round first man into the second place on her own side, the second woman moving up into first place.
B	1—2	First man and first woman cast up to the top, second couple moving down into their own place.
	3—4	First and second men go back-to-back with their partners.
	5—8	Circular-hey once round, partners facing (sk.s.).
	9—12	First couple leads down the middle, six steps (r.s.), and back again and casts down into the second place (sk.s.), second couple moving up into first place (progressive).

THE BRITAINS.

Longways for as many as will; in one part (10th Ed., 1698).

MUSIC.		MOVEMENTS.
		(Duple minor-set.)
A1	1—4	First man casts down and crosses over into second woman's place ; while second woman casts up and crosses over into first man's place.
	5—8	First man and second woman turn once-and-a-half round to places.
A2	1—8	First woman and second man do the same.
B1	1—4	The two men lead between the two women, cast off, meet and change places.
	5—8	First and second couples hands-four.
B2	1—4	The two women lead between the two men, cast off, meet and change places (progressive).
	5—8	First and second couples hands-four.

Mr. ENGLEFIELD'S NEW HORNPIPE.

Longways for as many as will; in one part (10th Ed., 1698).

MUSIC.		MOVEMENTS.
		N.B.—*The tune is in triple time, i.e., three steps to the bar.*
		(Duple minor-set.)
A	Bar 1	The first man turns his partner half-way round and changes places with her.
	2 – 4	First man, honouring his partner on the first beat of the second bar, joins both hands with her, moves backwards, pulling her after him, bears to his left and falls into the second place, second couple moving up into first place.
	5—8	Second couple does the same, first couple moving up into first place.
B	Bar 1	Partners face and join both hands. The first couple slips down three steps while the second couple slips up three steps, the second couple going between the first man and first woman and under their arms.
	Bar 2	Same again in reverse to places, the first couple passing between the second man and second woman and under their arms.

Mr. ENGLEFIELD'S NEW HORNPIPE—*continued.*

MUSIC.		MOVEMENTS.
		(Duple minor-set—*continued.*)
B	3—4	All fall back three steps and move forward to places, turning single as they do so.
	5—6	As in bars 1 and 2.
	7—8	First man and first woman cast down into second place; while second couple leads up into first place (progressive).

FOURPENCE HALF-PENNY FARTHING, or THE JOCKEY.

Longways for as many as will; in one part (10th Ed., 1709).

| 1 | 2 | 3 | 4 | • • • • |
| (1) | (2) | (3) | (4) | • • • • |

MUSIC.		MOVEMENTS.
		(Duple minor-set.)
A1	1—4	First man sets to second woman, moving forwards towards her, and falls back a double to place.
	5—8	First man turns second woman.
A2	1—8	Second man does the same to first woman.
B1	1—2	First man changes places with second woman.
	3—4	First woman changes places with second man
	5—8	First man crosses over and passes counter-clockwise round second woman into the second place on his own side ; while first woman crosses over and passes clockwise round second man into the second place on her own side.
B2	1—4	Second man crosses over and passes clockwise round first man into the first place on his own side ; while second woman crosses over and passes counter-clockwise round first woman into first place on her own side (progressive).
	5—8	First and second men turn their partners.

FROM ABERDEEN.

Longways for as many as will ; in one part (10th Ed., 1698).

MUSIC.		MOVEMENTS.
		(Triple minor-set.)
A	1—4	First man and first woman cast down into the second place, the second couple moving up into first place.
	5—8	First man turns his partner once-and-a-half round and falls back between and below third couple, his partner falling back between and above second couple.
B1	1—4	First man and third couple hands-three once round ; while first woman and second couple do the same.
	5—8	First man (having passed outside third man) hands-three with second and third men ; while first woman (having passed outside second woman) does the same with second and third women.
	9—10	First man and first woman meet and fall back, the man between and above second couple, the woman between and below third couple.

FROM   ABERDEEN—*continued.*

MUSIC.	MOVEMENTS.
	(Duple minor-set—*continued.*)
B2 1 4	As in B1, except that first man hands-three with second couple and first woman with third couple.
5—8	As in B1, except that first man hands-three with second and third women and first woman with second and third men.
9—10	First man and first woman turn half-way round and fall back, the man into the second place on his own side and the woman into the second place on her side (progressive).

MY LORD BYRON'S MAGGOT.

Longways for as many as will; in one part (11th Ed., **1701**).

1   2   3   4   . . . .

① ② ③ ④ • • • •

MUSIC.		MOVEMENTS.
		(Duple minor-set.)
A1	1—2	First man beckons to second woman who thereupon dances four steps towards him.
	3—4	The second woman, beckoning to first man, falls back to place, the first man moving forward at the same time.
	5—8	First man turns second woman.
A2	1— 8	Second man and first woman do the same.
B	1—4	The two men lead between the two women and cast off back to places.
	5—6	On the first beat of each bar all four clap their own hands; while on the second beat of fifth bar partners clap right hands, and on the second beat of the following bar, left hands.
	7—8	As in bars 5—6.
	9—12	First couple casts down into second place, second couple leading up into first place (progressive).

CHILDGROVE.

Longways for as many as will; in one part (11th Ed., 1701).

MUSIC.		MOVEMENTS.
		(Duple minor-set.)
A1	1—4	First man and second man side with their partners.
	5—8	First man and second man go back-to-back with their partners.
A2	1—4	The two men side; while the two women side.
	5—8	The two men go back-to-back; while the two women do the same.
B1	1—4	The two men turn once-and-a-half round and change places; while the two women do the same (sk.s.) (progressive).
	5—8	Partners turn (r.s.).
B2	1—8	First man and first woman go the Figure-8 through the second couple (r.s.), the first man crossing over, passing clockwise round second woman and counter-clockwise round second man, the first woman crossing over, passing counter-clockwise round second man and clockwise round second woman.

PORTSMOUTH.

Longways for as many as will; in one part (11th Ed., 1701).

| 1 | 2 | 3 | 4 | • • • • |

| ① | ② | ③ | ④ | • • • • |

MUSIC.		MOVEMENTS.
		(Duple minor-set.)
A1	1—8	First man goes the hey with first and second women (passing second woman by the right).
A2	1—8	First woman goes the hey with first and second men (passing second man by the left).
B	1—4	First man crosses over, passes counter-clockwise round second woman and returns to his place; while first woman crosses over, passes clockwise round second man and returns to her place.
	5—8	Circular-hey, three changes, partners facing.

THE QUEEN'S JIG.

Longways for as many as will; in one part (11th Ed., 1701).

MUSIC.		MOVEMENTS.
		(Duple minor-set.)
A1	1—4	First man sides with second woman.
	5—8	First man and second woman set and turn single.
A2	1—8	Second man and first woman do the same.
B1	1—2	First man changes places with second woman.
	3—4	First woman changes places with second man.
	5—8	The two men and the two women fall back two steps, cross over and change places (progressive).
B2	1—6	First and second couples right-hands-across.
	7—8	All turn single.

INDIAN QUEEN.

Longways for as many as will; in one part (11th Ed., **1701**).

$$\boxed{1} \qquad \boxed{2} \qquad \boxed{3} \qquad \boxed{4} \qquad \bullet \quad \bullet \quad \bullet \quad \bullet$$

$$\textcircled{1} \qquad \textcircled{2} \qquad \textcircled{3} \qquad \textcircled{4} \qquad \bullet \quad \bullet \quad \bullet \quad \bullet$$

MUSIC.		MOVEMENTS.
		(Duple minor-set.)
A1	1—4	First man and second woman move forward setting to each other and fall back to places, turning single as they do so.
	5—8	First man turns second woman.
A2	1—8	Second man and first woman do the same.
B1	1—4	First and second couples right-hands-across.
	5—8	First and second couples left-hands-across.
B2	1—4	Partners go back-to-back.
	5—8	Circular-hey, three changes, partners facing (progressive).

THE PRINCESS.

Longways for as many as will; in one part (11th Ed., 1701).

MUSIC.		MOVEMENTS.
		(Duple minor-set.)
A1	1—4	First and second men and first and second women fall back a double and move forward a double to places, turning single as they do so.
	5—6	First couple leads down into second place (w.s.), second couple casting up into first place.
	7—8	Partners set.
A2	1—8	All that again to places, second couple leading down.
B1	1—4	First man, joining both hands with his partner, falls back, pulling his partner after him, bears to his right and falls into second place (improper) ; while second woman, joining both hands with her partner, falls back, bears to her right and falls into the first place (improper).
	5—8	First couple leads up between second couple (w.s.) and casts off into second place (r.s.) (improper).
B2	1—6	First and second couples circular-hey, four changes, partners facing (sk.s.).
	7—8	Partners turn half-way round and change places (r.s.) (progressive).

CROSBEY-SQUARE.

Longways for as many as will; in one part (11th Ed., 1701).

1	2	3	4	. . . .
①	②	③	④	. . . .

MUSIC.		MOVEMENTS.
		(Duple minor-set.)
A	1—2	First man and first woman clap their own hands on the first beat of each bar, right hands on second beat of first bar and left hands on second beat of second bar.
	3—4	First couple casts off into second place, second couple moving up into first place.
	5—8	Second couple does the same.
B1	1—4	First man joining both hands with his partner, falls back, pulling his partner after him, bears to his right and falls into second place (improper) ; while second woman, joining both hands with her partner, falls back, bears to her right and falls into first place (improper).
	5—6	First man changes places with second woman, and first woman with second man.
B2	1—2	First couple casts down into second place, second couple leading up into first place (progressive).
	3—6	Partners turn.

THE ROUND.

Longways for as many as will; in one part (11th Ed., 1701).

| 1 | 2 | 3 | 4 | . . . . |

| ① | ② | ③ | ④ | . . . . |

MUSIC.		MOVEMENTS.
		(Duple minor-set.)
A1	1—4	First couple swings down the middle into the second place, second couple casting up into first place.
	5—8	Second couple swings down the middle into the second place, first couple casting up into first place.
A2	1—4	First and second men go four slips up and four slips down to places; while first and second women go four slips down and four slips up to places.
	5—8	Partners arm with the right.
B1	1—4	First and second men fall back a double and move forward a double to places; while first and second women do the same.
	5—6	All turn single.
	7—8	First man, joining both hands with his partner, goes four slips down the middle into second place; while second man and second woman go four slips up into first place, passing outside the first couple (progressive).
B2	1—4	First and second couples circular-hey, four changes partners facing.
	5—8	Partners arm with the right.

GREENWICH PARK.

Longways for as many as will; in one part (11th Ed., 1701).

MUSIC.		MOVEMENTS.
		(Duple minor-set.)
A1	1—4	The first couple leads up the middle (w.s.).
	5—8	The first couple leads back again and, releasing hands, passes outside the second couple into the second place (sk.s.), the second couple, in the last four steps, leading up into first place.
A2	1—8	The second couple does the same.
B1	1—4	First man and first woman cross over and cast down below the second couple.
	5—8	First couple swings up the middle into first place.
B2	1—4	Partners go back-to-back.
	5—6	All four clap their own hands on the first beat of each bar, partners clapping right hands on the second beat of fifth bar and left hands on the second beat of the following bar.
	7—8	The first couple casts down into second place; while the second couple leads up into first place (progressive).

THE JACK'S FAREWELL.

Longways for as many as will; in one part (11th Ed., 1701).

| 1 | 2 | 3 | 4 | • • • • |
| ① | ② | ③ | ④ | • • • • |

MUSIC.		MOVEMENTS.
		(Duple minor-set.)
A	1—2	First man and first woman face down and set to the second couple, moving forward.
	3—4	First man and first woman fall back to places, turning single as they do so.
	5—6	Partners set, moving forward.
	7—8	All fall back to places, turning single.
B	1—2	First and second couple hands-four half-way round.
	3—4	Partners change places (progressive).
	5—6	First man passes clockwise round second woman into the second place on the women's side; while first woman passes counter-clockwise round second man into second place on the men's side (sk.s.).
	7—8	First man and first woman turn half-way round.

SION-HOUSE.

Longways for as many as will; in one part (11th Ed., **1701**).

MUSIC.		MOVEMENTS.
		N.B.—*The tune is in triple time, i.e., three steps to the bar.*
		(Duple minor-set.)
A	1—2	First and second couples hands-four half-way round.
	3—4	The first woman changes places with the second man; while first man and second woman turn single.
	5—6	Hands-four half-way round.
	7—8	The first man changes places with the second woman; while the first woman and second man turn single.
B1	1—4	First and second men, joining inside hands, lead between the two women (w.s.) and cast off back to the same places (r.s.).
	5—8	Partners turn once-and-a-half round and change places (progressive).
B2	1—4	First and second women, joining inside hands, lead between the two men and cast off back to the same places.
	5—8	First man passes clockwise round second woman and returns to his place; while first woman passes counter-clockwise round second man and returns to her place.

BURY FAIR.

Longways for as many as will; in one part (10th Ed., 1698).

MUSIC.		MOVEMENTS.
		(Triple minor-set.)
A	1—4	First man casts down below third couple and stands between third man and woman, all three facing up.
	5—6	First woman casts down below second woman and stands between second man and woman, all three facing down.
	7—8	Opposites set to one another, *i.e.*, first man to his partner, second woman to third woman and second man to third man.
B	1—4	Second couple and first woman hands-three; while third couple and first man do the same.
	5—8	The same again, counter-clockwise.
C	1—8	First woman and second couple go the hey (first woman facing second man and passing by the right); while first man and third couple do the same (first man facing third woman and passing by the right), the first couple falling into the second place and the second couple into the first place (progressive).
D	1—4	First couple leads down through the third couple and casts up into second place.
	5—8	First couple leads up through the second couple and casts down into the second place.

THE QUEEN'S BIRTHDAY.

Longways for as many as will; in one part (12th Ed., 1703).

MUSIC.		MOVEMENTS.
		(Duple minor-set.)
A1	1—4	First man and second woman turn with right hands.
	5—8	First man and second woman turn with left hands.
A2	1—4	First woman and second man turn with right hands.
	5—8	First woman and second man turn with left hands.
B1	1—4	First man crosses over and passes counter-clockwise round second woman into the second place on his own side; while first woman crosses over and passes clockwise round second man into the second place on her own side, second couple moving up into first place (progressive).
	5—8	Partners turn.

DICK'S MAGGOT.

Longways for as many as will ; in one part (12th Ed., 1708).

MUSIC.		MOVEMENTS.
		(Duple minor-set.)
		N.B.—*The tune is in triple time, i.e., three steps to the bar.*
A	1—2	First man changes places with his partner.
	3—4	First couple leads down into second place ; while second couple casts up into first place.
	5—8	Partners fall back three steps, cross over and change places.
B1	1—2	Second man changes places with his partner.
	3—4	Second couple leads down into second place ; while first couple casts up into first place.
	5—8	Partners go back-to-back.
B2	1—4	First and second couples circular-hey, three changes, partners facing (progressive).
	5—8	Partners turn twice round.

JACK'S MAGGOT.

Longways for as many as will; in one part (12th Ed., **1703**).

1	2	3	4	• • • •
①	②	③	④	• • • •

MUSIC.		MOVEMENTS.
		(Duple minor-set.)
A1	1—8	First man crosses over and goes the hey with the two women (passing second woman by the right).
A2	1—8	First woman does the same with the two men (passing second man by the left).
B1	1—4	First and second couples right-hands-across.
	5—8	First and second couples left-hands-across.
B2	1—2	First man changes places with second woman.
	3—4	First woman changes places with second man.
	5—6	Hands-four half-way round.
	7—8	First couple casts off into second place, second couple leading up into first place (progressive).

THE COUNTRY FARMER.

Longways for as many as will; in one part (12th Ed., 1703).

| 1 | 2 | 3 | 4 | . . . . |
| 1 | 2 | 3 | 4 | . . . . |

MUSIC.		MOVEMENTS.
		(Duple minor-set.)
A	1—4	The first man, followed by his partner, casts off into the second place (improper), second couple moving up into first place.
	5—8	The second man, followed by his partner, does the same, first couple moving up into first place.
B1	1—2	First woman changes places with second man.
	3—4	First man changes places with second woman.
	5—8	First couple casts up into first place, second couple lead down into second place.
B2	1—4	First and second couples hands-four (sl.s.).
	5—8	Circular-hey, three changes, partners facing (progressive).

MY LADY FOSTER'S DELIGHT.

Longways for as many as will ; in one part (12th Ed., 1703).

MUSIC.		MOVEMENTS.
		(Duple minor-set.)
A1	1—4	First couple casts down into second place, second couple moving up into first place.
	5 8	First and second men turn each other ; while first and second women do the same.
A2	1— 4	Second couple leads down between the first couple and casts up into the same places.
	5 - 8	Partners go back-to-back.
B1	1- 4	First man casts up and crosses over into the first place on the women's side ; while second woman casts down and crosses over into the second place on the men's side (sk.s.).
	5 — 8	Second man casts down and crosses over into the second place on the women's side ; while first woman casts up and crosses over into the first place on the men's side (sk.s.).
B2	1— 4	First man and first woman lead down and cast up to places ; while second man and second woman cast up and lead down to places.
	5—8	First and second couples circular-hey, two changes, men facing and women facing (progressive) (sk.s.).

APLEY HOUSE.

Longways for as many as will; in one part (12th Ed., 1703).

MUSIC.		MOVEMENTS.
		(Duple minor-set.)
A	1—4	First and second men take hands, fall back a double and, releasing hands, move forward a double to places, turning single as they do so.
	5—8	First and second women do the same.
B	1—2	First and second couples right-hands-across half-way round.
	3—4	All turn single.
	5—8	Second woman, followed by first woman, and second man, followed by first man, cast down and form a line, four abreast, facing up, the first man and first woman on the outside.
C	1—4	Taking hands, all four move forward a double and fall back a double, the first couple falling into the first place (improper) and the second couple into the second place (improper).
	5—8	First man and first woman cast down into the second place, cross over and change places; while second man and second woman lead up into the first place, cross over and change places (progressive).

OLD NOLL'S JIG.

Longways for as many as will; in one part (12th Ed., 1703).

1	2	3	4	. . . .
①	②	③	④	. . . .

MUSIC.		MOVEMENTS.
		(Duple minor-set.)
A1	1—2	First man and first woman change places, turning single as they do so.
	3—8	They set to one another and cast off into second place, second couple moving up into first place.
A2	1—8	The second couple does the same.
B	1—4	First and second couples right-hands-across (sk.s.).
	5—8	First and second couples left-hands-across (sk.s.).
C	1—4	First man crosses over, passes clockwise round second woman and returns to the same place, jumping on the second beat of the fourth bar; while first woman crosses over, passes counter-clockwise round second man and returns to the same place, jumping on the second beat of the fourth bar.
	5—8	First man and first woman cast off into the second place, turn each other half-way round and change places, second couple leading up into first place and turning in like manner (progressive).

FY, NAY, PRITHEE JOHN.

Longways for as many as will; in one part (12th Ed., 1703).

☐1	☐2	☐3	☐4	■ ▪ ◂ ●
①	②	③	④	▴ ▪ ◂ ■

MUSIC.		MOVEMENTS.
		(Duple minor-set.)
A1	1—4	First and second men and women fall back two steps, and move forward six steps, partners changing places without turning round.
	5—8	First and second couples hands-four half-way round, facing outward.
A2	1—8	Second man and second woman (now at the top) cross over, cast down, cross over again below first couple, cast up to the top and turn each other (sk.s.).
B	1—2	All four clap their own hands on first beat of first and second bars, partners clapping right hands on second beat of first bar, and left hands on second beat of second bar.
	3—4	Second couple casts down into second place, first couple leading up.
	5—6	As in bars 1 and 2.
	7—8	First couple casts down into second place, second couple leading up into first place (progressive).

UP WITH AILY.

Longways for as many as will; in one part (12th Ed., 1703).

| 1 | 2 | 3 | 4 | • • • • |

| ① | ② | ③ | ④ | • • • • |

MUSIC.	MOVEMENTS.
	N.B.—*The tune is in triple time, i.e., three steps to the bar.*
	(Duple minor-set.)
A1 Bar 1	Second man and first woman move into line and stand on either side of first man. All three take hands and face second woman.
2—3	They move forward three steps to second woman and fall back three steps.
Bar 4	Second man and first woman return to places.
5—6	First man casts down into second place; while the two women turn single and the second man moves up into first place, turning single, counter-clockwise, as he does so.
A2 Bar 1	Second man and second woman move into line and stand on either side of first woman. All three take hands and face first man.

UP WITH AILY—*continued.*

MUSIC.		MOVEMENTS.
		(Duple minor-set—*continued.*)
A1	2—3	They move forward three steps to first man and fall back three steps.
	Bar 4	Second man and second woman return to places.
	5—6	First woman casts down into second place; while the two men turn single and the second woman moves up into first place, turning single, clockwise, as she does so.
B	1—2	First man goes back-to-back with his partner.
	3—4	First couple casts up into first place; while second man and second woman lead down into second place, turning single on the last three steps, the man clockwise, the woman counter-clockwise.
	5—7	First and second couples hands-four.
	Bar 8	First couple casts down into second place; while second man and second woman move up into first place, turning single as they do so (progressive).

NOWILL HILLS, or LOVE NEGLECTED.

Longways for as many as will; in one part (14th Ed., 1709).

| 1 | 2 | 3 | 4 | • • • • |
| ① | ② | ③ | ④ | • • • • |

MUSIC.		MOVEMENTS.
		(Duple minor-set.)
A1	1—8	First man goes the hey with second couple (first man passing second woman by the left).
A2	1—8	First woman goes the hey with second couple (first woman passing second man by the right).
B1	1—4	First man moves counter-clockwise round his partner, she standing still; while second woman moves clockwise round her partner in like manner.
	5—8	First woman moves clockwise round her partner; while second man moves counter-clockwise round his partner.
B2	1—4	The two men take hands, fall back a double and move forward a double to places; while the two women do the same.
	5—8	First and second couples circular-hey, three changes, partners facing (progressive).

HUNT THE SQUIRREL.

Longways for as many as will; in one part (14th Ed., 1709).

MUSIC.		MOVEMENTS.
		(Triple minor-set.)
A1	1—8	The first man, followed by his partner, heys through the second and third men (they standing still), passing outside second man, and returns to his place, his partner moving across to her place after passing round third man.
A2	1—8	The first woman, followed by her partner, heys through the second and third women, passing outside second woman, and returns to her place, her partner, after passing round third woman, moving across to his place.
B1	1—2	First man changes places with second woman.
	3—4	First woman changes places with second man
	5—6	Hands-four half-way round.
	7—8	First couple casts down into second place, the second couple moving up into first place (progressive).
B2	1—4	First and second couples circular-hey, four changes, partners facing.
	5—8	Partners turn (sk.s.).

THE GEUD MAN OF BALLANGIGH.*

Longways for as many as will; in one part (10th Ed., 1698).

1	2	3	4	• • • •
①	②	③	④	• • • •

MUSIC.		MOVEMENTS.
		(Duple minor-set.)
A1	1—4	First man and first woman lead down between second couple and cast up to places.
	5—8	First and second men, joining inside hands, lead between the two women (w.s.) and cast off back to places (sk.s.).
A2	1—4	Second man and second woman lead up between first couple and cast down to places.
	5—8	First and second women, joining inside hands, lead between the two men (w.s.) and cast off back to places.
B1	1—4	First man sets to second woman, moving forward, and falls back to his place, turning single.
	5—8	First woman sets to second man, moving forward, and falls back to her place, turning single.
B2	1—4	First and second couples hands-four half-way round.
	5—6	Partners set.
	7—8	Partners change places (progressive).

* To be danced to the tune of "Hunt the Squirrel" (Set 11).

ROUND O.

Longways for as many as will; in one part (14th Ed., 1709).

1	2	3	4	. . . .
(1)	(2)	(3)	(4)	. . . .

MUSIC.		MOVEMENTS.
		(Triple minor-set.)
A1	1—4	First man and first woman set to each other and cast down into second place, second couple moving up into first place.
	5—8	The first woman crosses over and passes clockwise round second man into the second place on the men's side; while the first man crosses over and passes clockwise round the third woman into the second place on the women's side (sk.s.).
A2	1—4	First man casts up above second woman (sk.s.), and moves down the middle into the second place on his own side (r.s.); while the first woman casts down below third man (sk.s.) and moves up the middle into the second place on her own side (r.s.) (progressive).
	5—8	First man and first woman set to each other and then fall back four small steps.
B	1—2	Second couple faces third couple. Second and third men set to one another moving towards each other; while second and third women do the same.

ROUND O— *continued.*

MUSIC.		MOVEMENTS.
		(Triple minor-set—*continued.*)
B	3—4	All four fall back, turning single as they do so.
	5—8	First man and first woman the whole-gip, clockwise, facing and waving their hands (hopping step ; four hops on right foot, four on left).
C	1—4	First woman goes back-to-back with second man ; while first man does the same with third woman.
	5—8	First woman goes back-to-back with third man ; while first man does the same with second woman.
D	1—8	The three men go straight-hey (second man facing first man and passing by the right) ; while the three women do the same (second woman facing first woman and passing by the right) (sk.s.).

MR. BEVERIDGE'S MAGGOT.

Longways for as many as will; in one part (11th Ed., 1701).

1	2	3	4	. . . .
①	②	③	④	. . . .

MUSIC.		MOVEMENTS.
		(Duple minor-set.)
		N.B.—*The tune is in triple time.*
A1	1—2	First man and first woman cross over and change places.
	3—4	First man goes back-to-back with second woman; while first woman goes back-to-back with second man.
	5—6	First man, facing down, turns single and then turns second woman with the right hand half-way round; while the first woman turns single and then turns second man with the right hand half-way round.
	7—8	First man and first woman turn with left hands, moving up to places.
B1	1—2	First man and first woman cross over and cast down into second place (improper), second couple moving up into first place.
	3—4	First and second men go back-to-back with their partners.

MR. BEVERIDGE'S MAGGOT—*continued.*

MUSIC.		MOVEMENTS.
		(Duple minor-set—*continued.*)
B1	5— 8	First couple standing between second couple, all four take hands and move up six steps and fall back six steps, first couple falling into first place (improper), second couple into second place (proper).
B2	1—6	First couple goes the Figure-8 through the second couple, first man crossing over, passing clockwise round second man and counter-clockwise round second woman, second woman crossing over, passing counter-clockwise round second woman and clockwise round second man.
	7—8	First man and first woman cross over and cast down into second place, second couple moving up into first place.

GENERAL INDEX.

PARTS I—VI.

The figures in parentheses refer to *Country Dance Tunes*, Sets 1—10.

THE COUNTRY DANCE BOOK.—PART V.

THE GRAND PROMENADE. *p.* 24.

Lines 4 & 5. Substitute "(right over left) and all move round the circle eight steps counter-clockwise, men on the inside (*i.e.*, on the left of their partners)."

Line 8. For "Still holding hands" read "Without releasing hands."

Line 10. Insert "the circle" after "move round."

Line 15. Insert "the circle" after "dance round."

THE LITTLE PROMENADE. *p.* 24.

Lines 3 & 4. Insert "the circle" after "once round," and add "men on the inside (*i.e.*, on the left of their partners)."

GOING DOWN TOWN. *p.* 30.

At end of last paragraph add "The men are now in their own places."

UNWIND THE BALL YARN. *p.* 34.

Lines 3 & 4, on p. 35. For "fourth man and first woman" read "fourth woman and first man."

THE COUNTRY DANCE BOOK.—PART VI.

THE SHEPHERD'S DAUGHTER. *p.* 83.

Music.		Movements.
C	5—8	Substitute " (r.s.) " for " (sk.s.)."

SIEGE OF LIMERICK. *p.* 96.

B	9—12	Add " in the last bar."

FROM ABERDEEN. *p.* 101.

A		For " 1—4 " read " 1—2."
		For " 5—8 " read " 3—8."
	Page 102	For " Duple minor-set " read " Triple minor-set."

DICK'S MAGGOT. *p.* 116.

A	Bar 1	First man changes places with his partner.
	Bar 2	First couple leads down into second place, etc.
	3—4	Partners fall back three steps, etc.
	Bar 5	Second man changes places with his partner.
	Bar 6	Second couple leads down, etc.
	7—8	Partners go back-to-back.
B	1—4	First and second couples circular-hey, etc.
	5—8	Partners turn twice round.
		N.B.—Omit the repetition of B music in the accompaniment.

UP WITH AILY. *p.* 123.

A1 (p. 124)	Read " A2."

MR. BEVERIDGE'S MAGGOT. *p.* 130.

A1	5—6	For " half-way " read " once " in both instances.
	7—8	For " moving up to places " read " half-way round to places."